Your
Horoscope
2022

....

Taurus

21 April – 21 May

*igloo*books

igloobooks

Published in 2021
First published in the UK by Igloo Books Ltd
An imprint of Igloo Books Ltd
Cottage Farm, NN6 0BJ, UK
Owned by Bonnier Books
Sveavägen 56, Stockholm, Sweden
www.igloobooks.com

0721 001
2 4 6 8 10 9 7 5 3 1
ISBN 978-1-80022-529-9

Written by Belinda Campbell and Denise Evans

Designed by Simon Parker
Edited by Suzanne Fossey

Printed and manufactured in China

CONTENTS

Introduction 5

The Character of the Bull.............................6

Romantic Relationships 11

Family and Friends.....................................18

Money and Careers 20

Health and Wellbeing.................................22

Daily Forecasts for 2021............................25

Daily Forecasts for 2022............................51

People Who Share Your Sign 141

INTRODUCTION
. . . .

This 15-month guide has been designed and written to give
a concise and accessible insight into both the nature of your
star sign and the year ahead. Divided into two main sections,
the first section of this guide will give you an overview of your
character in order to help you understand how you think,
perceive the world and interact with others and – perhaps just
as importantly – why. You'll soon see that your zodiac sign
is not just affected by a few stars in the sky, but by planets,
elements, and a whole host of other factors, too.

The second section of this guide is made up of daily forecasts.
Use these to increase your awareness of what might appear on
your horizon so that you're better equipped to deal with the
days ahead. While this should never be used to dictate your
life, it can be useful to see how your energies might be affected
or influenced, which in turn can help you prepare for what life
might throw your way.

By the end of these 15 months, these two sections should
have given you a deeper understanding and awareness of
yourself and, in turn, the world around you. There are never
any definite certainties, but with an open mind you will find
guidance for what might be, and learn to take more control of
your own destiny.

THE CHARACTER OF THE BULL

. . . .

Steady and grounded, Taurus is a fixed earth sign that the rest of the zodiac can surely rely on. Slow and steady is how this Bull wins the race. Those who have a Taurean in their life should learn to not expect fast results. But boy, when a Taurean delivers, it is likely to be a stunning result. Taurus is known for being one of the most multitalented signs in the zodiac calendar, with a keen eye for the aesthetic. Some of the best artists, makers, writers and creators the world has ever known have been Taureans, such as Salvador Dalí and William Shakespeare.

Lovers of the finer things in life, Taureans may want to surround themselves with beautiful soft furnishings, sparkling jewellery, alluring artwork and other riches. Likewise, Taureans will gorge themselves on equally fine wines and delicious foods. The lure of beautiful things can be constant for Taureans, and whilst this can feel like a cruel fate when money is not free flowing, it can be an added motivation for doggedly pursuing their goals. Perseverance, after all, is what this sign is also best known for. The Taurean love of beauty does not always stop with material things. This springtime sign has a deep connection with Mother Earth. Hiking and working outdoors to enjoy the beauty of the world or finding ways to preserve and protect nature's wonders can be integral to Taureans. The associated colour for Taurus is green and whilst this may be linked to a love of nature, it can also be an indicator of a green-eyed monster that lies within. Possession is a key characteristic of the Bull and whilst this usually relates to material objects, Taureans can sometimes be guilty of treating their loved ones as possessions too.

Jealousy, superficiality and stubbornness are the potential downsides of the talented, nurturing and tenacious Taurean.

THE BULL

Strong and masculine, the Bull inside of Taurus has plenty of charge and direction – there's a reason why everyone aims for the bullseye! The Bull is capable of charging when necessary, similarly Taureans can roll up their sleeves and deliver solid and fast results when life demands it. However, like the Bull, Taureans are more suited to a slower pace of life. Stopping to smell the flowers, taking time to relax in green pastures; this instinct of appreciating Mother Earth should be indulged whenever possible. This sign has an utmost appreciation for the finer things in life, but too often this is translated into material objects and wealth alone. What Taureans value and benefit from most is a long meander through woodlands or reading a good book in the park. Taureans can be accused of being bullish or stubborn, particularly when change is happening that they are uncomfortable with, or if it feels too great or sudden. In ancient Greek mythology, Zeus transformed himself into a white bull and whisked his love, Europa, to Crete. Zeus's bull has many similarities with Taureans; romantic, tenacious, sometimes possessive and often mystical. Ultimately, the friends and family of a Taurean should feel safe with the Bull by their side, an utmost nurturing and protective symbol that slowly but steadily provides for loved ones.

VENUS

Venus is named after the Roman goddess of love and beauty, so it is no surprise that these very two things govern Taurus. Taureans can happily spend a night at the theatre, ballet or opera, nestled in plush, red velvet seats and revelling in some of the finest displays of beauty and culture with a glass of fine wine. Slaves to their senses, Taureans can take immense pleasure in music, art, dining and, last but not least, physical activities. Encouraged by Venus, tactile Taureans can have a reputation for being sensual lovers. Considered to be some of the most attractive people, guided by their desires and ruled by the planet of love, romance is likely to play a huge role in the life of a Taurean.

ELEMENTS, MODES AND POLARITIES

Each sign is made up of a unique combination of three defining groups: elements, modes and polarities. Each of these defining parts can manifest themselves in good and bad ways and none should be seen as a positive or a negative – including the polarities! Just like a jigsaw puzzle, piecing these groups together can help illuminate why each sign has certain characteristics and help us find a balance.

ELEMENTS

Fire: Dynamic and adventurous, signs with fire in them can be extroverted. Others are naturally drawn to them because of the positive light they give off, as well as their high levels of energy and confidence.

Earth: Signs with the earth element are steady and driven with their ambitions. They make for a solid friend, parent or partner due to their grounded influence and nurturing nature.

Air: The invisible element that influences each of the other elements significantly, air signs will provide much-needed perspective to others with their fair thinking, verbal skills and key ideas.

Water: Warm in the shallows and sometimes freezing as ice, this mysterious element is essential to the growth of everything around it, through its emotional depth and empathy.

MODES

Cardinal: Pioneers of the calendar, cardinal signs jump-start each season and are the energetic go-getters.

Fixed: Marking the middle of the calendar, fixed signs firmly denote and value steadiness and reliability.

Mutable: As the seasons end, the mutable signs adapt and give themselves over gladly to the promise of change.

POLARITIES

Positive: Typically extroverted, positive signs take physical action and embrace outside stimulus in their life.

Negative: Usually introverted, negative signs value emotional development and experiencing life from the inside out.

TAURUS IN BRIEF

The table below shows the key attributes of Taureans. Use it for quick reference and to understand more about this fascinating sign.

SYMBOL	RULING PLANET	MODE	ELEMENT	HOUSE
The Bull	Venus	Fixed	Earth	Second

COLOUR	BODY PARTS	POLARITY	GENDER	POLAR SIGN
Green	Neck and throat	Negative	Feminine	Scorpio

ROMANTIC RELATIONSHIPS

. . . .

The slow and steady nature of Taureans means that quick-fire love affairs are unlikely. Instead, they are more likely to find romance blossoming from a friendship, or pursue someone who has been on the outskirts of their life for a while. A sense of security is important to Taureans for their relationships to succeed. An insecure Taurean can turn into a jealous creature that is guilty of suffocating a relationship in a misguided effort to greedily possess a partner. Perhaps the most important lesson for this Bull is to learn how to share a partner's time rather then attempt to dominate it. This is not always an easy task for Taureans, particularly if they come from a small family and are less used to sharing their loved ones. Yet it's an important lesson to practise regularly to keep significant others happy. As with most things, sharing can be easier said than done. Communicating emotions is essential to any successful relationship, and will lead to deeper affection between Taureans and their loved ones.

An ideal partner for a Taurean is one that feeds both the desires and the stomach! Food is essential to the happiness of a Taurean, so the trick to keeping the relationship sweet may be to keep those snack drawers well stocked. A partner who cooks is one that a Taurean will be more inclined to try and keep hold of. Whilst Taureans love to be doted on and thrive on affection from their spouse, they should not be pandered to. A good partner for a Taurean should maintain a level of autonomy and not be tempted to indulge in letting their lover take ownership over them – even if it makes for an easier life! A Taurean's equal should fight to keep their individuality, but also display patience and love. In return, a Taurean will show fierce loyalty and love, for better or for worse.

ARIES: COMPATIBILITY 3/5

The Taurean Bull and the Arean Ram may look like two headstrong individuals doomed to clash, but they actually have the potential for a sensual relationship. Whilst their passions for each other are intense, this couple will need to keep a reign on their potential stubbornness and desire to win in order to form a lasting relationship outside of the sheets. The Taurean can be guilty of possessiveness, which the free spirited Arean may struggle with. However, with a joint love of nature and being outdoors, this passionate duo could find their Eden together.

TAURUS: COMPATIBILITY 4/5

This love can be one for the ages. When a Taurean falls for a Taurean, it may be slow and steady as is their usual way or it can be love, and lust, at first sight. These two romantics will shower each other with affection and reciprocate the dedication and loyalty that each deserves. Not one to give up, both Bulls will stand by the other through thick and thin. Should they not see eye to eye, these two are capable of fighting with terrifying passion but will hopefully find that making up is always more fun.

GEMINI: COMPATIBILITY 2/5

Three may prove to be a crowd. The duality of a Geminian, characterised in their twin symbol, can make a Taurean feel uneasy in starting a romantic relationship with this sign. The earth sign of Taurus mixed with airy Gemini may not be an easy joining, but if Taurus can budge on their fixed ways then love could grow happily here. Gemini's good communication skills will mean that they should hopefully understand quickly the needs of a Taurus and provide the love and security that Taureans crave in a partner. Communication, trust and flexibility should be this couple's mantra.

CANCER: COMPATIBILITY 5/5

Placed two positions apart on the zodiac calendar, a Cancerian and Taurean share a bond that can feel like home. The Cancerian's frequent displays of love are deep and clear, like two names carved into a tree! The intensity of the Taurean's affection, mixed with the Cancerian's head-over-heels approach, can see these two lovers running to the altar and settling down with babies – not always in that order. Here are two signs that will do anything for each other, and will usually prefer their own little party of two.

LEO: COMPATIBILITY 3/5

Leo is ruled by the Sun and Taurus by Venus; this star and planet are never further away than 48 degrees from each other. The love that these two share is solidified in their sometimes-stubborn commitment to one another. The Lion and Bull are both fixed signs and this can be their undoing in a long-term relationship when neither one is willing to compromise. Both will shower each other with affection and admiration, and will boost each other's self-esteem and be a positive influence in their careers. This couple should just be careful to not let their egos get in the way.

VIRGO: COMPATIBILITY 3/5

A Taurean and Virgoan can make for a real power couple. The Taurean's dogged approach to fulfilling goals and the Virgoan's practical and busy mind will see this pair securing a successful future together. The Virgoan can appear overly critical and may end up hurting the Bull's feelings unintentionally. Ruled by Mercury, the planet of communication, the Virgoan can be very attuned to the Taurean's needs and will try to fix any problems within the relationship. These two earth signs will likely share many things in common and can form lifelong companionships, even if a whirlwind romance isn't in the stars.

LIBRA: COMPATIBILITY 4/5

Both ruled by the planet Venus, the love that a Taurean
and Libran share can be a thing of beauty. Their shared
appreciation of culture and aesthetics will have romance
blooming quickly. Wedding bells might ring in both the
Taurean and Libran's ears, and planning for the big day could
begin sooner rather than later. The Libran's airy indecisiveness
can be a point of contention for the grounded Taurean, and
these two won't be without their disagreements. However, the
Libran's diplomacy will help to resolve issues and have them
striving for harmony once more.

SCORPIO: COMPATIBILITY 5/5

Scorpio and Taurus are each other's opposites on the zodiac
calendar, so therefore cosmically share a special relationship
both in their differences and similarities. The element of
Taurus is earth and Scorpio's is water, which usually will
mean that both partners will provide something that the other
desperately needs. Love and passion are both driving forces for
these two. Scorpio has the reputation for being the amorous of
signs and Taurus the most beautiful, so a physical relationship
should be strong here. Whilst this couple will no doubt enjoy
a close and passionate partnership, their tendencies towards
more negative emotions will need to be kept in check.

SAGITTARIUS: COMPATIBILITY 2/5

A Sagittarian is ruled by the planet Jupiter, which is associated with luck – something that a Taurean doesn't always believe in. Whilst the Sagittarian values new experiences, the Taurean prefers familiar, safer comforts. The biggest struggle that this fire and earth couple may have is the Sagittarian's need for freedom, and the Taurean's tendency towards possessiveness with a partner. A claustrophobic atmosphere should be avoided, and freedom actively given in this relationship. They must learn from one another; both by admiring the faster gallop of the Centaur, and equally by appreciating the steady plod of the Bull.

CAPRICORN: COMPATIBILITY 3/5

A Capricornian and Taurean in love are loyal and true to each other. These two earth signs value hard work, and are driven by their need to enjoy the fruits of their labours. The home that these two could build together will likely be full of beautiful and expensive objects, with a couple of prized cars jewelling the garage. Whilst both will have dreams of marriage, the Capricornian is the more traditional one and will probably approach the subject first. The Taurean should try to inject joy and fun into the relationship to teach the Capricornian how to enjoy the lighter side of life.

AQUARIUS: COMPATIBILITY 1/5

A Taurean and Aquarian aren't an obvious match on paper, and it's unlikely they will be paired on a dating website. The core differences between these two makes a romantic spark unlikely, but should not be ruled out. The Aquarian is partly ruled by the planet Uranus, symbolising rebellion and change – often the Taurean's worst nightmare. For the easy life-seeking Taurean who likes what they know, the Aquarian's wanderlust can be hard to keep up with. These two signs are both fixed and have the potential to make each other stronger if they remain open to change.

PISCES: COMPATIBILITY 3/5

A Taurean and Piscean are capable of having a highly sympathetic and understanding love together. The practical-minded Taurean should encourage the dreamy Piscean to live out fantasies and work hard, for everyone's benefit. In return, the Piscean will shower the Taurean in waves of love and gratitude for all the support and encouragement. However, the Piscean would be wise to not saturate the relationship emotionally and spoil the Taurean. With the Piscean being a water sign, the Taurean can feel the nourishing effects this sign has on its earth element, and the life that these two can grow together is one well worth living.

FAMILY AND FRIENDS

· · · · · · · · · · · · · · · · · ·

Just as Taureans are dedicated to sticking to their goals, the same steadfast dedication is given to maintaining relationships with friends and family. Taureans want to see loved ones succeed, and will try to offer unfailing support mentally, physically and financially if they can. Positioned under the second house in the zodiac calendar, Taurus has a strong influence with possessions and money. Taureans are not ones to spend all their hard-earned wealth on just themselves, instead they are likely to want to share their fortunes with loved ones. From picking up a cheque for dinner to paying for extracurricular activities for their children, Taureans are generous with their love, time and money.

A Taurean home will clearly display signs of success, wealth and a love for beautiful and opulent design. From decorative throws and pillows, to the artwork hanging on the walls (that may or may not be a Taurean original), to the grand piano taking centre stage, the Taurean home will likely be a stunning display of the beauty in life. Beauty-loving Librans and homemaking Cancerians will value the stylish home that Taureans are capable of building, and can provide some of the most appreciative and kindred of friendships or relatives.

A key characteristic of Taureans is their focus on possession, which can lead them to become workaholics in their desire to be the affluent provider for their family. When it comes to family, it's important for Taureans to remember that the people for whom they are providing are more important than what they are providing. Despite their weakness toward possession, what Taureans are more reliably known for is their unmoving loyalty and stability, both key attributes for building a happy family home. If a Taurean befriends or is related to another Taurean, their relationship will have the strong bones for forming some of the most reliable and steady relationships that the zodiac calendar knows.

Be careful of upsetting Taureans because they can hold a grudge for years and years. They would do well to learn to forgive any friends and family they feel have done them an injustice, if they want to keep that person in their life. Taureans should ask themselves this question: is it more important to hold on to this grudge or to hold on to this relationship? Taureans choose their friendships wisely and will usually be unwilling to let go of their investment in it, even if the friendship has soured or become too toxic to remain close. Taureans should learn to live and let live, and move forwards from any disagreements that they have with their family and friends. If a Taurean chooses to keep a friendship after a falling out, it should be based on forgiveness with an unclouded look towards a happier, shared future.

MONEY AND CAREERS

· · · · · · · · · · · · · · · · ·

Being a particular star sign will not dictate certain types of career, but it can help identify potential areas for thriving in. Conversely, to succeed in the workplace, it is just as important to understand strengths and weaknesses to achieve career and financial goals.

The mode of Taurus is fixed, rather than cardinal or mutable, which in career terms can mean that once Taureans decide what their career path is, they will stubbornly stick with it until they achieve their goal ambitions. Which career path to take may not always be clear, particularly as they are known for being multitalented. Whilst a career choice may be undecided, belonging to the second house in the zodiac calendar representing wealth will mean that dreams of money and fortune will no doubt be a driving force for all Taureans. A career in finance, such as investment banking, could be a satisfying job, as they will enjoy watching their investments grow over time. High-risk decisions won't be appealing to Taureans. Rather, a steadfast investment is something that will likely attract them to parting with their hard-earned money.

Whilst Taureans may be naturally good at a job in finance, the more negative characteristics associated with this sign, such as greed and being overly materialistic, may mean that this avenue is best avoided to help keep these traits at bay. A more grounded career, influenced by this sign's earth element, may be complementary to a happy work life. The gradual and sustainable process of growing plants or vegetables lends itself to the slow-paced Taurean, so perhaps a career in horticulture would be well suited. Taureans' appreciation of beauty may lead to work in conservation, appealing to their nurturing side and their love of Mother Earth. Whether it is through full-time work or a leisurely activity, being in nature will have a positive and calming effect, and offer balance and perspective.

Ruled by Venus, the planet of beauty, the sign of Taurus has great potential with pursuing a career in the arts. Some of the best-known artists, including Salvador Dalí and William Shakespeare, are Taureans. Taureans strongly value security, and might struggle with the uncertainty of success, financial or otherwise, that a life in the arts can offer. This dislike for unsteady work and working for no immediate money are things that arty Taureans will need to overcome. However, their determination to hone their craft by stubbornly working towards their goals day by day can mean the bright lights of fame and success will be the ultimate pay-off. Taureans are known for not just appreciating beauty but also for being beautiful themselves, so perhaps a career in acting or fashion, like Taurean supermodel Gigi Hadid, may prove fulfilling.

As with family, colleagues cannot be chosen. Therefore, it can be advantageous to use star signs to learn about their key characteristics and discover the best ways of working together. As co-workers, Leonians can have a positive influence on Taureans by encouraging them to make bolder choices. However, Taureans may find Leonians difficult bosses, as neither the Bull nor the Lion is likely to admit defeat graciously. Taureans are multitalented in the workplace, and share many skills with other signs; from their problem-solving initiative that links them with practical Virgoans, to the resolute ambition they share with desirous Scorpians. These appealing attributes, together with their calm and patient nature, make Taureans liked and valued by their colleagues.

HEALTH AND WELLBEING

....

Being a lover of the finest food and drink, Taureans can sometimes struggle with keeping their weight down. Not ones to deny themselves the luxury of eating out at fine restaurants, those calories can add up as high as their bill. And what's dinner without dessert? By making more meals from scratch at home, Taureans will be more aware of the ingredients going into their favourite foods. Taureans are known for their pre-planning and organisation skills. By utilising these positive traits in the kitchen, Taureans can prepare healthy meals ahead of time, and ensure that they are eating a more balanced diet.

Taurus rules the throat and neck and, like the Bull, it is often a Taurean's strongest area. Perhaps that is why this sign is known for being home to some of the most famous singers of all time, from James Brown to Ella Fitzgerald and Adele. Even if a Taurean does not enjoy singing, it may be beneficial to take extra care of this area by always wearing a scarf in the colder months, and avoiding drinking too much alcohol that could aggravate the throat.

Bulls are strong with a stocky build, and Taureans often find success in weightlifting or gymnastics. However, earth is the element that guides Taurus and so physical exercise is likely to be·enjoyed more so in Mother Nature than it is in the confines of a man-made gym. Walking is a wonderful form of regular and gentle exercise that Taureans can enjoy at an adjustable speed that is comfortable for them. Not only will walking or running outdoors help with maintaining a level of physical health, it will also make sure that they stay connected to nature where they feel their calmest.

Maintaining a healthy mind is just as important as listening to what the body needs. Taureans can be stubborn and unforgiving of people that they feel have wronged them. If fixated on, this negativity can be extremely harmful for Taureans and may even manifest itself in physical pain, such as a tight neck and shoulders. By practising forgiveness and letting go of negative emotions, Taureans should find that they are much happier and healthier, and are able to refocus on what brings them joy. Exercise that centres on bringing balance to the mind as well as the body, such as yoga or t'ai chi, will help calm the aggravated Bull.

Jealousy can also be another internal sore sport for any Taurean. Whilst it is a normal emotion experienced by most, Taureans can feel its sting too often in their relationships, and it may become a real cause of pain if left to fester. By questioning why these feelings of jealousy arise, Taureans can then work towards nipping those negative emotions in the bud.

Taurus

....

DAILY FORECASTS
for 2021

OCTOBER

· · · · · · · · · · · · · · · · ·

Friday 1st

You are already in the mood for the weekend. The current energy lifts your spirits and you may even suggest or attend a party. Connections from the Sun and Mars in your health and duties sector make you feel good. The jobs are done, so now it is time to let your hair down.

Saturday 2nd

You might come up against some opposition from people in charge or elders. You will push on through this and disregard them. A useful connection from your ruler helps you to persuade others to join in the fun. Don't overdo it, as this may make enemies.

Sunday 3rd

Today you may be doing small jobs for people. Offering your services may win you brownie points. This could just be as simple as some DIY or a selfless act of kindness. People will look up to you today and you won't let them down.

Monday 4th

Expression and creation may be hard to access today. The Moon is eager to help you show the world what you've got but Neptune sitting opposite makes it a little foggy. This could be a day when things simply do not go your way. You may find it hard to make a start, and possibly shouldn't anyway.

Tuesday 5th

This afternoon you make more headway and can look objectively at projects or passions you are involved in. The joy returns and you are able to discern what did not work and transform it. Look at how the balance between work and free time lies. You may need to make changes here.

Wednesday 6th

A new moon in your health and duties sector allows you to make decisions about the way forward. The Sun and Moon sit with Mars and you may feel emotionally drained or fired up. Use this as a moment to pause and reflect before moving on.

Thursday 7th

Pluto is now direct and likes that you have decluttered some areas of your life. Travel plans are now possible again. This evening you are inclined to spend time with a lover or, if single, to spoil yourself with luxuries. Your ruler enters your intimacy sector, so prepare for a sultry time.

Friday 8th

Ego is on a high today. You have a need for release or physical exercise. You may not do things by the book today, as you feel a little rebellious. Shadow material could surface from your unconscious for you to deal with. Do not fear it.

Saturday 9th

Friends and lovers clash today. You can't please everyone. This is a difficult day and you need an outlet for your energy. Words of passion or anger need to be checked as this is still Mercury retrograde time and today, he is in the heat of the Sun.

Sunday 10th

Saturn now turns direct and the pressure in your social circle is relieved. People who have been exposed as fake are no longer in your groups. Venus is asking that you explore the width and depth of your close relationships and where you are joined in financial obligations with someone.

Monday 11th

A bit of luck may come your way today as the Moon makes a nice connection to Jupiter. This is likely to be in the workplace but will also be connected to something radical and unusual. Continue to explore the larger world; you may just learn something new.

Tuesday 12th

One step at a time, remember. If you have a metaphorical mountain to climb today, use your knowledge of being an earth sign and be methodical, determined and steady. Progress may feel slow, but you are doing the right thing. Look at all angles and make strong decisions on the way up.

Wednesday 13th

Today is another day where you might recycle an old idea or habit. You can be too fixed in your own theories and find it difficult to accept another. The planetary energy is here to help you do that today. Transform lead into gold and be pleased with your result.

· · · · · · · · · · · · · · · · ·

Thursday 14th

As the Moon enters your career sector, you are emotionally
drawn to review your status. Are you where you want to be?
Could you add a small goal to your work prospects? You may
feel anxious or rebellious and this might cause some unrest.
Watch your words today.

Friday 15th

Any emotional state you are already in will be exaggerated,
today. Jupiter likes to make everything bigger and he connects
with the Moon now. You may feel like the luckiest person alive
and overlook the small details. Mind that Jupiter does not
inflate your ego too much.

Saturday 16th

It's the weekend and once more the Moon sits in your social
sector. However, you may feel at a loss of what to do. Perhaps
there are no invitations for you today. The urge to connect
may not be satisfied today; use this time to connect with
spirit instead.

Sunday 17th

A busy day in the heavens reflects your mindset today.
Your mind is overloaded with fantasy thinking. Dreams
and visions appear intrusive and you wish to switch off.
Have some downtime but try not to use alcohol or other
unhealthy crutches, as they will take you to a place which
is more frenzied.

Monday 18th

At last, Mercury turns direct and you begin to get some clarity. Any health issues you may have noticed in the last few weeks should now be addressed. The plans in your head, your vision board and your search for a new focus will now become easier to access.

Tuesday 19th

The Moon opposite newly direct Mercury means that you have an emotional heart-to-heart with yourself. Forgive yourself for any time you felt in jeopardy. Don't go down the self-blame route as it is now closed. Introspection will give you valuable insights into your conditioned behaviour.

Wednesday 20th

Today you feel tired and lack motivation. Stick with it, as this will pass. A full moon in your dreams sector may highlight the need for you to spend time alone. It may also show you that you have too many things on the go and your mind cannot hold them all.

Thursday 21st

The Moon now sits in your own sign and you may feel rather selfish. Like a small child, you will be prone to tantrums if you do not get your own way. There might be a struggle with someone in authority who attempts to pull you out of this mood.

Friday 22nd

There might be more conflict today. You could be stamping your feet and raging at what you perceive as a personal injustice. The two ruling planets of your opposite sign are arguing, and you will see some of your darker side as your shadow is triggered. This needs to be healed now.

Saturday 23rd

The Sun enters your relationship sector, and this can go two ways for you. Either this can be a warm and healing time with a special person, or it could show you exactly where you project your shadow onto another. What you dislike about someone could be something inside you.

Sunday 24th

Conversations around money and value will be on the agenda today. How you place value onto material things will be up for discussion. As a Taurus you are more prone to loving money and possessions, but not all people do. It is time to look at and review any joint investments.

Monday 25th

A fantasy or illusion you have been harbouring may now come crashing down around you. It could be that you see the real person instead of the image you have projected onto them. By the time evening comes, you will be craving for the old and familiar feeling of days past.

Tuesday 26th

You need to be around those who can nurture you. Home comforts or family favourite meals are just the things to nourish you today. You could be licking your wounds after a reality check. Mothers or female friendships are helpful and will offer a good place for you to recover.

Wednesday 27th

If you are finding it hard to express your basic need, then tune into your intuition. Listen to what it is telling you. You'll need to excavate your deep, dark areas and take away your safety blanket for now. This could be an emotionally difficult day for you.

Thursday 28th

As the Moon shifts into your family sector, you should find yourself feeling tired but safe. Security means a lot to you now and being with family and loved ones can help. Your ruler, Venus, connects with Jupiter and sends you luck and love. Harmony within you can be restored now.

Friday 29th

Although you have now regained some joy, there will always be something or someone who will try and bring you down. You may be on shaky ground with a family member. Sibling rivalry is possible. The good thing is that you are able to get things off your chest now.

Saturday 30th

Mars enters your relationship sector which is likely to stir things up. Mars, associated with energy and drive, is the ruler of this sign, so you could be in for a wonderful evening with a partner. However, increased energy can turn to aggression and you could easily end up with an evening filled with arguments. Watch this space.

Sunday 31st

The Moon returns to your creative sector. As this sector also deals with falling in love, perhaps you have rekindled a relationship or made apologies for upsets made during Mercury retrograde. Planetary energy is easier now and relating with others should be more straightforward. Be kind and selfless, and you will be rewarded.

NOVEMBER

· · · · · · · · · · · · · · · · · ·

Monday 1st

Are you fighting the mists of Neptune? Sometimes you are asked to go with the flow but keep a tow line connected to land. At these times, it is difficult for you to stay in the moment. A tendency to over-drink, over-eat or generally over-indulge is likely now.

Tuesday 2nd

Mundane jobs need your attention. If you can get to grips with things that need doing, then you can free up some time for health or leisure activities. You might struggle with someone trying to control how you spend your time. Saturn allows you the grace to deal with this with kindness.

Wednesday 3rd

The Moon meets up with Mercury today. Filtering information that comes your way may bring about an emotional response. You may also be more inclined to go over the top with these emotions. Triggers happen for you to recognise and deal with. Look at how you habitually react and respond.

Thursday 4th

A new moon in your opposite sign offers a chance to deal with your darker side. Issues concerning relating, sex, death and rebirth are good starting points. Aggression or passion will be high today. Remember that the other person has feelings too. Be mindful and remember boundaries.

Friday 5th

Mercury now enters your relationship sector. He will assist you in having those deep conversations about the meaning of life and the universe. Venus also moves today; she will now enter your travel sector. Perhaps these two signify a travel opportunity to mysterious lands to explore with your partner.

Saturday 6th

Today has lighter energy. You may be looking back at things you have enjoyed in the past. Again, travel is the theme. You might yearn to revisit a place where you have felt at home. Might this be a good opportunity to introduce a partner to a piece of your past?

Sunday 7th

Your mind is still wandering off to distant lands. You could satisfy this by watching documentaries, reading books, or looking at websites which showcase a land and people you have an affinity with. Be careful not to get trapped in a fanciful illusion now as this may disappoint when reality kicks back in. Keep it real.

Monday 8th

The Moon and Venus met up tonight and they now add a feminine touch to any travel plans you might have. You have some unusual ideas, and feel fired up thinking about how your senses will be touched by countries and philosophies you had not previously considered. Plan your itinerary.

Tuesday 9th

Think about how you can have a shared experience. You are very good at going it alone but now your wish is to have someone to enjoy it all with. Plan ahead, take small steps and get things in motion. You have the leadership skills to do this.

Wednesday 10th

Today is not so easy and it seems that any route you take could have a dead end. You might get frustrated and run the risk of being argumentative. The Moon is making some bad connections to difficult planets. The only saving grace you have today is that you can talk about it.

Thursday 11th

Something is growing or building in your consciousness. You want to get it all out but now is not the time. This evening, Jupiter lends you some of his expansiveness and whatever is eating at you gets bigger. Hold it a little while longer.

Friday 12th

Today would be a good day to look to your tribe and ask for advice and personal experiences similar to your plans. Your ruler helps you to balance what is good and bad information. Stay in that holding space and consider all your options. Friends and social groups are invaluable now. Connect and learn.

Saturday 13th

Planetary energy lifts at first but, once more, you are lost in a sea of fantasy. Your mind is now swimming with far too much information. It's likely that you'll blurt out your latest ideas and look a fool. Knowing you, you'll feel hurt but won't change anything.

Sunday 14th

Social groups can be overwhelming now. You wish you had
not spoken too soon. However, your friends mean well and
want you to understand that. This afternoon, you welcome
the chance to switch off and be alone with your thoughts and
dreams. They have become too precious for you to lose.

Monday 15th

In your own little world, you consider your responsibilities and
come back down to earth. You needed to do this in your own
time. Even though this goes against your nature you know
that, if it is not dealt with, there'll be trouble down the line.

Tuesday 16th

Watch out for ego clashes today. The Sun's in your opposite
sign and the Moon is in your dreams sector; your partner
could win. You might have truth and justice on your side from
Jupiter, but the planet of control Pluto is against you. Take it
on the chin and retreat if you must.

Wednesday 17th

This morning, the Moon shifts into your sign. Unfortunately,
this does not bring relief. Saturn restricts your movement,
and Mars and Uranus stand off. This makes for a lot of
tension. Something's going to blow. Are you the volcano
in this scenario?

Thursday 18th

Your feelings are very close to the surface now. Although there are helpful connections to Neptune who can soften and dissolve arguments, there are harder connections from the Moon in your sign to the more volatile planets. Today, it might be better to stay in bed. This war is not over yet.

Friday 19th

A full moon in your sign is the perfect spotlight for the recent troubles. You can clearly see now how things came to this. People will be pointing the finger; let it not be at you. Venus softens any further disruption and Pluto helps change it into something better.

Saturday 20th

Your finances and possessions come under scrutiny today. You may be tempted to over-spend as a way to lift up your spirits, but this is not the answer. Saturn asks you to spend responsibly and you'll be rewarded in another way. Treat yourself to a good old Taurean dining experience instead.

Sunday 21st

The influence of Neptune today means that you need to keep as grounded as possible. Self-indulging as a way to cover up wounds that need healing is not the answer. As Jupiter is involved here too, anything you do or feel today might get out of hand.

Monday 22nd

Come morning, your emotional body needs home comfort
and nurturing. The Sun now warms up your intimacy sector
and Venus and Mars make a good connection. Find someone
that you love or have high regard for and share a hug or two.
Offloading to a special person works wonders.

Tuesday 23rd

Although the Moon sits opposite your ruler, Venus, you still
manage to have an emotionally satisfying day. Irritability and
frustration become calm. This could be by family members.
Mothers, in particular, have a big role to play today. Listen to
older women and appreciate their wisdom.

Wednesday 24th

When being nurtured, make sure that you aren't in fact
being manipulated. Make messages short and sweet. Late
this afternoon, you should feel re-energised. Mercury is at
the final degree of your relationship sector and asks that you
make sure all is well before he goes adventuring in your deep
intimacy sector.

Thursday 25th

Today, cooperation between people comes easy. You will
want to express yourself loudly but consider holding back in
order to give another a chance to shine. In doing this, you
are shining a stronger light and leading by example. You may
reminisce with family members.

Friday 26th

Maybe you just cannot resist being the centre of attention today. You gave the spotlight to someone else and now you are snatching it back. This is likely to make you very unpopular. Jupiter is right opposite and watching as you inflate your ego in a way which displeases him.

Saturday 27th

The Moon drifts back into your creative sector. You may have a bruised ego now and wish to make amends. However, whatever comes out of your mouth now might not be good enough. Emotions and self-awareness are out of sync. Give up and try again another day.

Sunday 28th

Today is another one of those days where you just want to switch off and be alone. Try doing this in a constructive way. Do you have any paperwork or admin that needs attention? Today is perfect for editing, filing and other general admin tasks. Start the new week with a tidy mind and home space.

Monday 29th

This morning the Moon enters your health and duties sector. Get your head down and stuck into work. This will ease the tension you have built up within you. Mercury is in the heat of the Sun so your mind could be busy with whatever task you set it to today.

Tuesday 30th

Your responsibilities come first today. Venus may try to cajole you into fantasy land, but you resist. A lot of good planetary connections to Saturn help you get the job done and with time to spare. A session at the gym will finish the day off well. Treat yourself to a healthy smoothie, too.

DECEMBER

....

Wednesday 1st

Your relationship sector is highlighted today. Neptune, the planet that can dissolve established structures, goes direct now. You may have some clarity in relationship concerns. Suddenly, all is not as it once was and anything that was once solid may now begin to crumble. Let it go.

Thursday 2nd

Your sense of self might feel threatened today as a Scorpio Moon throws light on your shadow. You may feel resistance to this, but Neptune asks that you go with the flow. What you resist will persist. Triggers are the key to your unresolved business. You might feel uncomfortable, but you will grow.

Friday 3rd

You are after something and determined that you will have it. This could be a night in with a partner as the Moon meets up with hot-headed Mars. Aggression can also appear now under this influence. This afternoon you feel more fired up to get out and about. Use that Mars energy to do something exhilarating.

Saturday 4th

The final new moon of the year asks that you set intentions around wider exploration. You may have a secret impulse to explore esoteric subjects or other cultures. Planning a holiday is a great thing to do under this Moon. Mercury will help you do a little research.

Sunday 5th

Today has just the right feel for a splendid Sunday afternoon. Spending time away from home could lift your spirits. Take the first steps for any new projects you have lined up. Today will also be a good day to do those jobs that need to get done. Lighter energy brings you good fortune and a spring in your step.

Monday 6th

Due to the Moon making easy connections to difficult planets, your emotions are controlled and stable. There is an element of surprise today. You may be changing your mindset about someone you once thought was important to you. Be kind and let them go with love.

Tuesday 7th

The Moon meets up with Pluto today and you may feel a little manipulated. However, other influences suggest that you are more likely to be changing a poor situation into a better one. Your career is illuminated when the Moon shifts this afternoon. Take time to consider your work prospects.

Wednesday 8th

In the workplace, there can be some conflict which may cause you to lose face. Luck might not be on your side today and you may end up eating humble pie. Those in authority demand respect and like a child you are reluctant to give it. The rebel in you is riled.

Thursday 9th

Unfairness angers you today, but you might be meeting up with someone who you hope can change this. There will be a lot of conversation, but do make sure that you are getting your facts right or you will be known as a gossip or rabble-rouser. Ask trusted friends for advice.

Friday 10th

Under a Moon in your social sector, you end the weekend with your tribe. You need to be with like-minded souls who understand your principles. Social media groups can support your views but be careful that you're not doing this to stroke a bruised ego.

Saturday 11th

Something which you once believed strongly may fall apart before your eyes. Your inner child may be hurt by this. Today you are not sure what you is truth and what is not. This is a passing phase, so don't fret. By late evening, your ruler soothes you and makes you more stable.

Sunday 12th

Today you are best advised to spend time alone with your thoughts. Anger is bubbling under the surface. You need to process recent events and changes. For a Taurus, this can be difficult. A short dive into the underworld of your psyche is necessary. You may even find some pearls.

Monday 13th

Two planets change sign today. Mercury enters your travel sector and wants to research future vacations. Mars marches into your sex, death and rebirth sector, looking for action. He will now cull anything that is not serving you in this area. He may also bring a few secrets with him.

Tuesday 14th

Stay in your own mind for a short while longer. Something has stirred within you and this needs addressing. When the Moon moves into your own sign today, this will be on the dissecting table. You may not like what you see, but you must do something with it.

Wednesday 15th

You are likely to blow a fuse today. Take note of what triggers you again. Another face-off with an authority figure or elder of your family is possible. You mind find yourself reaching back into the past and bringing forward a skill set you have not used for some time.

Thursday 16th

Today you have a better idea of the inner work you need to do. The outer planets, Neptune and Pluto, are connecting to the Moon in your sign and helping you. You get a clearer sense of self and understand the need for change. Self-love will be your motivator now.

Friday 17th

The next two days are an opportunity to organise your finances before the holiday season kicks off. You need to catch up with messages or small chores over the weekend. Saturn is pleased that you are being sensible today. Well done.

Saturday 18th

Venus, your beautiful ruler, goes retrograde today. At these times, it's important to review where you place value and how you bring peace and harmony. You may see a face from the past or a love affair might fall apart. Venus will be hanging around in your travel sector, causing a few upsets.

Sunday 19th

A full moon in your money sector advises you to look at where you may have over-spent this year, as it may be taking its toll now when you need it. A family day will be nurturing as an early seasonal get-together satisfies your emotional needs. Start preparing for the festivities now.

Monday 20th

Mercury and the Moon both connect to Uranus in your sign. This signifies early surprises as pleasant energy flows easily. You might have to curb what you say if one of those surprises is not to your taste. You must choose whether to speak from your head or your heart.

Tuesday 21st

It is the winter solstice and the longest night. This is the perfect time to hunker down with all your favourite comfort foods and entertainment. Someone may try to take control, but you can let them know there is no need. You know best how to nourish yourself.

Wednesday 22nd

Being with family brings out your inner child. You feel happy to be with those who know you best and where you can truly express yourself unfiltered. You may come across some opposition regarding breaching another's boundaries. Leave them alone and enjoy them for who they are.

Thursday 23rd

Jupiter is at the last degree of your career sector. If you have not already shut down for the holidays, check if there is anything crucial that you need to complete now. The planet of joy would like you to enjoy the season without extra worries.

Friday 24th

A busy day in the heavens means that last minute shopping or arrangements are highly likely. There is much to do and the Moon's connections to disruptive planets isn't going to make it easy. Watch that temper and pull your weight today; there is too much at stake.

Saturday 25th

If there is a female who tries to take control today, let them. Venus has met Pluto in her retrograde and she will not be happy feeling powerless. As she is your ruler, you will probably feel this intensely. You might find it difficult to relax, so try to keel indulgences to a minimum.

Sunday 26th

Beautiful connections from the Moon mean that today is far more relaxing. The hard work has been done and you can kick back and enjoy yourself. There is a balance of duties by this evening and you feel satisfied that all has gone well. Well done for doing your part.

Monday 27th

You feel energised and buoyant today. You may have had a responsible festive season so far and Saturn is pleased with you. Use the energy from Mars to ensure you stay focused and visit friends and relatives you have missed. This could also be a great day for intimate connections.

Tuesday 28th

Today is not likely to be so easy for you. The Venus retrograde might already be causing a fuss in your outgoing travel sector. There may be arguments or simply disagreements, as not everyone is on the same page today. Mind what you say with sensitive people and back down if you must.

Wednesday 29th

The Moon in your relationship sector asks that you spend some time with a special person. As usual, this can mean that you are triggered, but for good reason. Jupiter enters your social sector today. Prepare for a year where your friendships and groups get much bigger and more active.

Thursday 30th

Time spent with a partner will be deep and mysterious now.
Conversations can border on the taboo but do not offend. If
you are a night owl, you will feel a little more anxious and
possibly judged in the late hours. Do not take it too personally.

Friday 31st

There is only one way to end the year for you. Your emotions
and passions are in sync so grab your partner and reminisce
on what went well in 2021. Get those travel brochures out and
expand your horizons. Set your sights on making next year a
big adventure.

Taurus

....

DAILY FORECASTS
for 2022

JANUARY

. . . .

Saturday 1st

Happy New Year and welcome to 2022. Your emotions may be deep and intense. There may be something from your subconscious which is niggling you. Social groups may be presenting a challenge and you could be reassessing the value of certain friendships. A love affair from the past may have resurfaced for your attention.

Sunday 2nd

A new moon allows you to set goals and intentions for the year concerning travel and learning. Your social status and career can also be themes to consider. Business talks and networking will be high on the agenda when you are back in work. Good causes and fresh ideas may attract you now.

Monday 3rd

A ghost from the past could play on your heartstrings today. This may be a long-distance love or a place you yearn to revisit. Pay attention to your dreams and visions now. They may include groups of people you have not been involved with before.

Tuesday 4th

You may feel livelier and chattier today. A new idea or way of approaching your work might be exciting and you could be eager to get this off the ground. However, remember to listen to elders or bosses and take on board any lessons or words of wisdom they might have for you.

Wednesday 5th

Today you may be more outgoing than usual. You have a passion for getting out and about, exploring or deepening your knowledge of other countries and philosophies. This energy may exhaust you if you aren't careful, but may also fire you up to follow your dreams, wherever they may lead.

Thursday 6th

A spiritual group may provide you with the connection you need. This may feel uncomfortable to you at first as you feel exposed and vulnerable. Learn to go with the flow more and be accepting of other's differences. Being suspicious will hinder any progress here. Your emotions may be hard to handle today.

Friday 7th

If you need to be alone, find the time to do so. You may have unwanted attention from your friendship circle or from the past. Hold on to what you know and don't let subtle manipulation overwhelm you. If you think something is too good to be true, then it probably is.

Saturday 8th

Communication is the key to understanding your mind's most private workings. Your self-talk may be negative, but listen carefully and you may hear a voice which is supportive and encouraging. Your best-laid plans are done when you are alone and have time to process them.

Sunday 9th

Past loves or desires may fill your mind today. Your dreams could present images you would rather not see. It's possible that you are thinking about a holiday to a place which is dear to you. Is this place no longer there? Might you have burned bridges and now seek to return?

Monday 10th

Friendship groups may clash with your own interests now. Make sure that their values are in line with your own. You may be seeing a difference in energies and evaluating if this is worth your effort. Do something you love this evening and indulge in some self-care.

Tuesday 11th

You have a restlessness which will not go away today. You may wish to try exercise or using your mind to get to the bottom of a problem. If today feels like an uphill struggle, take a step back and slow down. Try again when the energy is better for you.

Wednesday 12th

Practical activities might help you get focused and stay in control. You may have sympathy for someone and wish to reconnect differently. It's possible that you can see another perspective on a past issue and wish to remedy mistakes you have made. Do this with sincerity or don't bother.

Thursday 13th

You could be impulsive today both with words and actions. You may need to filter what you say, especially in the workplace. Decisions regarding your future goals come into your awareness, but as they aren't urgent, don't spend too much energy on them. Make your speech clear when talking to elders.

Friday 14th

Mercury turns retrograde today. Do all the necessary checks. Back up all devices, double-check travel plans and get ready for a bumpy ride in your career zone. You may be rethinking a strategy or plan to enhance your work status, but don't sign anything until this is over.

Saturday 15th

Your energy could be low today, so take a day off and enjoy staying safe at home. Communications via email or messaging may feed your soul while your body rests. Good food and company will suffice if this is what you desire, but so will an ice-cream and duvet day.

Sunday 16th

Look out for something which is hidden coming to light today. There may be a revelation or two. This can be shocking, and you will need to consider how you feel about it. Although it may not involve you directly, it could have an unexpected emotional impact. Stay away from mind games and be careful not to say something untoward.

Monday 17th

A full moon may make you fearful and insecure. You may be taking attacks on someone from the workplace personally when they aren't. This is not about you, but your response will show you parts of your psyche which need to change, evolve, and be healed.

Tuesday 18th

Uranus moves directly into your sign today. You may notice that his prolonged stay has been causing havoc with your sense of security. You have some months now to evaluate that. Find your voice and speak from the heart. Take care though, your family may still treat you like a child.

Wednesday 19th

You could come across as an unfiltered bossy-boots today. You could clash with authority figures and let your ego get the better of you. This won't look good. Use your outspokenness to put matters right and not make them worse. You may be narcissistic today and leave a bad impression.

Thursday 20th

Everything you do at work is being observed. Make the most of the sun moving into this area and let it shine positively on you. You can make a difference now if you put the effort in and become more empathic and altruistic. Unconditional service will be good for you.

Friday 21st

Creativity and romance are highlighted today. You might surprise yourself and others by paying attention to detail. Healing is possible with a ghost from the past and this may be the way to get closure on something once and for all. Passions may be high or volatile.

Saturday 22nd

It may be hard to hold on to your inner compass today. When something feels aligned with your core values, it feels good. Today, it doesn't feel right. It may be that you need to make a positive change or permanent ending, and this grieves you more than you care to admit.

Sunday 23rd

Listen carefully for any subtle messages today. You need not say anything at all. Dreams, chats, gossip or casual conversation may need to be clarified for meaning. A last-minute push may be needed on an intense project. Probe a little deeper to find out what this is.

Monday 24th

Mars enters your travel zone now. You may find that there is a way you can combine your work with trips abroad. This could be just the thing you need to satisfy your travel itch and learn new things at the same time. Look into this as you might find it is extremely valuable.

Tuesday 25th

Your one-on-one relationships may need your attention now. Remember not to upset the status quo and take extra care when communicating. Misunderstandings may lead to bigger problems. Past loves or money-making ventures might be on your mind and you wish to investigate this further.

Wednesday 26th

Surprises and revelations may show you that your old behaviour patterns have caused many problems. However, today you may be dealing with something in a completely new way and you will notice you achieve better results. This will also be in line with your core values and personal truth.

Thursday 27th

Change comes easily today as you can wave goodbye to something from the past. Your heart may be thinking about expanding your horizons, but you also know your limits. Find a workable way to satisfy your need for travel, connection and a sense of belonging to a family or tribe.

Friday 28th

Putting your ideas to the boss may be beneficial today. However, remember that Mercury is telling you not to make commitments just yet. Plant seeds and let them grow. You could feel out of sorts tonight and will benefit from alone time, doing what helps you relax.

Saturday 29th

Stay away from power struggles today. You could see passive-aggressive behaviour, or you could be the one trying to manipulate a situation. Expect your hot-headed passion to boil over today. This could be good if you intend it in a positive way. If not, it could be catastrophic and harmful.

Sunday 30th

If you have come to a reconciliation point with someone, don't be tempted to tip the balance in your favour. Leave it as it is. You may need to put others' needs first and drop the ego. This will do you good when you realise how you have made another feel safe.

Monday 31st

It may be exceedingly difficult for you to stay out of trouble today. This could take place at work and might damage your status if you get involved. Think of the future, think where you would like to be considered for more responsibility and think about how you would feel if you lost out.

FEBRUARY

....

Tuesday 1st

A new moon allows you to set your career goals for the next six months. If they can involve you breaking free from an old way of doing things and being selfless, you will have a good chance of success. Talk to your elders and ask for all the options.

Wednesday 2nd

You may wake thinking this is going to be a challenging day. However, as the day progresses you might merge and connect with like-minded people who offer you choices. Your energy may pick up as will your motivation and you might get more done than you first anticipated.

Thursday 3rd

A day of bright ideas and great strategies awaits you. Tap into the energy offered by your ruler Venus in a powerful position. Integrating both your feminine and masculine faculties now can improve your chances of climbing the corporate ladder and broadening your mind. Breaking free from tradition can bring innovative rewards.

Friday 4th

Mercury turns direct today. You may now have a clear image of how you would like to progress and expand this year. Don't jump into anything just yet, check in with your inner compass and to ensure it is still aligned. Elders and bosses have great things to teach you now.

Saturday 5th

You might find it difficult to unwind this weekend. Your mind may be occupied with plans for the year. This evening would be best spent with someone who has wisdom and experience you can learn from. You may wish to incorporate their values into your own system.

Sunday 6th

If you resist something, then it will only keep coming back for attention. You may be having concerns about how change will affect you. The only way to know is to implement it. If you wish to grow and learn this year you must allow change to transform you.

Monday 7th

The Moon in your sign may make you feel invincible today. It's easy to connect to the natural flow now as you feel the benefit of it in your body, and this you trust. You are more likely to call on friends and social groups to support you in your quest for wholeness.

Tuesday 8th

You may feel restricted by your responsibilities and this might slow you down. This is temporary and by afternoon you can get back on track easily. It may be that you simply need to look at things from a different perspective to discover that the blockage is just an illusion.

Wednesday 9th

Networking could possibly help you to gather your resources and lay foundations for this year. Speak to others who can give you financial advice. Choices may be hard, but you will decide the right thing eventually. Onwards and upwards is a great motto, but lay the ground rules down first.

Thursday 10th

You may not feel so optimistic today. This might be because you are overwhelmed with information that needs sifting and sorting. Try not to discard anything until you're sure of its value in your goals. File things away for later. Look at the wider picture, but remember your limitations and responsibilities.

Friday 11th

Today would be a good time to talk to those above you and get them on board with your plans and ambitions. It doesn't hurt to plant seeds where they may have a chance of growth. You may hear something to your advantage which will help you complete a project.

Saturday 12th

Mars and Venus are getting closer. For you, this means that your mental and emotional faculties could merge and give you a more empathic and passionate outlook on life. You may be able to balance physical urges with love and harmony. This will become evident in your career and world adventures.

Sunday 13th

You might struggle with insecurity now and consider packing in your ambitions. Talk to those who know you best. Be open and honest with them and listen to what they say. You may have a need for safety and comfort which is conflicting with a need to protect your values.

Monday 14th

This morning might present a challenge and make you feel intimidated. However, as the day moves on you may find your voice and stand up for yourself. What may have seemed like an attack may have been coloured by your doubts and worries about not being good enough.

Tuesday 15th

An urge to rebel or stir up trouble will need to be quashed now. You are being offered a chance to make peace with your foes and gather new allies in your quest to bring passion and love to your travel and work plans. Don't bite the hand that feeds you.

Wednesday 16th

Your ruling planet, Venus, meets her lover today. You might see any battles between the sexes calling a truce. A full moon also highlights your family area and your role within it. You can be creative or romantic over the next few days and maybe have a meet up of your own.

Thursday 17th

Remember to look out for others today. Your inner rebel may find a good cause to attach to. This could satisfy your needs to investigate corruption and bring an end to anything unfair or dishonest. Look to your social groups and work colleagues for extra support.

Friday 18th

Grounded energy suits you. Today you may do things which are practical and methodical. Check in with your health or schedule an exercise regime. These may have been neglected recently and you should put them right. You are your best self when seeing to your bodily needs. Your body will thank you.

. . . .

Saturday 19th

The focus switches today and you would benefit from more mental activity. You could be sorting, filing and organising. A tidy workspace can freshen up your mind and let ideas flow easier. Check your planner and make sure that you haven't overlooked anything which has a deadline coming up.

Sunday 20th

There may be some unrest now and you are likely to feel this in your mundane daily duties. You could be resenting how much time they take up and distract you form your personal goals. Take it easy today and do what needs to be done. Be responsible and mature.

Monday 21st

The week begins with an intense atmosphere. You could be ending something with some reluctance to see it go. Deep investigations of your relating patterns may crop up for you to deal with. A partner may be seductive and intoxicating. You may be attracted or repulsed by this. Or both.

Tuesday 22nd

A secret or taboo love affair may be floating your boat at the moment. However, it could raise some issues within you which can be ugly. You may like closeness but on your own terms, and someone may be probing too deeply for your liking. Make your boundaries known.

Wednesday 23rd

You may be thinking of past relationships now and comparing them to current ones. This is unfair unless you are learning from past mistakes. Still, you wish to go deeper but may need a guide or friend to help. Travelling may take you away from reality but is short-lived.

Thursday 24th

Today you may be very outspoken and stand up where others fail to do so. You may see this in your career or in your wider groups. Be careful that you don't clash with someone in charge. Look at your boundaries and those of others. Be respectful and don't cross that line.

Friday 25th

Your own dreams may take a back seat today. They may even be starting to look unattainable. Don't change anything as this is just a passing phase which allows you to review your progress so far. Travel and research seem to attract you now, but maybe a documentary will suffice.

Saturday 26th

There is lovely, easy energy for you today. Grounding activities or practical work may bring out the genius in you. Building, gardening or even cooking up a tasty treat for a loved one will feed your soul. You may wish to impress someone from your social groups.

Sunday 27th

This is a very romantic day. If you desire something, go after it and it will be yours. This doesn't have to be a person but could be anything you are passionate about. Transformational energy is available to you, so use it wisely and you could turn lead into gold today.

Monday 28th

Love and romance have you looking at the past and future. How much would you like to invest in this? At first, you may feel resistant, but when you have had more time and more discussions, you may notice that your passion could be the best thing for you right now.

MARCH

· · · · · · · · · · · · · · ·

Tuesday 1st

A feeling of stuckness blocks your path today. You may try pushing and pushing until you have a breakthrough. However, this could result in an egotistical outburst and make you look childish. If this is more of a problem-solving energy, you will achieve more by working with a trusted colleague.

Wednesday 2nd

Today may be emotionally intense. Relationships are tested and could be going through major changes. A new moon in your social arena may make you tearful or spiritually inclined to seek a soul family. Talk with those who know their stuff and can give you good advice.

Thursday 3rd

The planetary energy continues to be unstable. Hold on to your inner compass and follow the way which is right and moral. It might be a bumpy ride, but by evening you could have a revelation and know exactly how to progress. There may be no turning back where relationships are concerned.

Friday 4th

The energy dips into your most private thoughts. You would benefit from time alone in order to lay down plans for yourself. A busy mind may be distracting, but be mindful that this isn't an avoidance tactic. Material from your psyche is making itself aware so it can be healed.

Saturday 5th

You may feel a shift in focus now. A sense of urgency regarding relationships, travel and exploring may intrude on your private time. You may have a spiritual moment of enlightenment and realise a few home truths. Social groups are supportive but may also be the trigger.

Sunday 6th

Mars and Venus move into your career zone together. You could now move with an air of integrated wholeness into the workplace. You may worry if you can keep this up. Stay true to yourself and beware of false behaviour giving you bravado. If it doesn't feel right, it isn't right.

Monday 7th

Helpful energy allows you to problem solve and be optimistic. You may have more empathy and connection with others today, which makes you feel good. Take care though as this could easily turn into something from which you alone benefit as you may thrive off the attention and status it brings.

Tuesday 8th

Today you may receive more of an idea of where your career is headed. Finances feature highly and you may be negotiating a long-term investment or bonus. Security in terms of money and housing concern you. Take steps to gather your resources. Be your best self at work and it will be noticed.

Wednesday 9th

There are now four planets in your career zone. You may experience this as hectic energy, but you may also thrive on it. Deadlines might be stacking up and you could have little time left in the day for yourself. Connect or network with a group before you miss your chance.

Thursday 10th

Social groups can be more useful to you now. They can be there for you when you need to rant or let off steam. Be mindful who you choose to confide in as you may be inclined to gossip or preach about something you don't understand fully.

Friday 11th

Conversations with family can be soothing for your soul now. You may have a softer edge which you show only when with your tribe. This is your safe place where you feel protected and nurtured. Check in with relatives, particularly siblings if you need to offload your worries.

Saturday 12th

You can unwind more today and shed some of the burdens of your work identity. Always try to see the need to be real because keeping up an appearance you don't feel could be exhausting you. Take off the mask and let yourself breathe. Nurture your inner child to calm your soul.

Sunday 13th

Your inner compass shines brightly today. As you relax, you may see more ways of attaching yourself to what your heart desires. You may need to let something go and make space for new growth to happen. If you are a hoarder, it's time for a clear out.

Monday 14th

Returning to the working week may make you resentful as you feel that part of your work is out of alignment with your basic needs and truths. Tension can build and you could be at risk of having a tantrum. Find your safe place and let off that steam without harm.

Tuesday 15th

A clash with authority is possible today. You could be speaking up for yourself and going against the status quo in your groups or workplace. You may be challenged or put in your place. Alternatively, you may choose to do nothing and be the observer who watches how this plays out.

Wednesday 16th

Getting creative might to help to release tension. For you, this may involve organising, filing or decluttering messy corners. With a new space to work from you can create a healthy spot and let energies flow through unrestricted. One small clearance in your home may lift your spirits and give you a sense of achievement.

Thursday 17th

You may dismiss the urge to chatter and dream in favour of creative, romantic or mundane pursuits. You may be more emotionally attached to an immediate result than a long-term passion today. If this works for you, go ahead. Leave your big dreams for another time.

Friday 18th

Today's full moon highlights how you have been working on your health, hobbies, romance and obligations. Something may be complete. Get in touch with your body and listen to its needs. A health problem may have resurfaced or become more urgent. See to your own needs first and others later.

Saturday 19th

Your mind may be doing overtime today. There's a lot of mental energy around which can make you think and strategise better. You may need help to solve a problem and this could cause some tension. However, by evening you could feel satisfied and pleased with yourself.

Sunday 20th

The spring equinox offers you a chance to pause before jumping into action. As a Taurus, this usually means that you spend time in your head before laying foundations. Take a couple of days to sift through the many layers of your psyche and pull up any hidden treasure from there.

Monday 21st

Discussions within your social groups could be very lively now and will need extra time to process. You may now discover a spiritual path which suits you. However, a restless day awaits you and you may struggle to get everything done to the correct standard. Share the responsibilities with others.

Tuesday 22nd

A partner may provide you with food for thought. They may delve deeper into your thoughts and see your potential. It could annoy you to accept that they might be right, but you are willing to be guided on a journey of personal growth and development.

Wednesday 23rd

Your mood is very outgoing today. From your passion and drive to your quest for harmony, you take on board everything offered. Your inner compass has some instructions for you. This requires you to listen, communicate and learn from someone in your social circle. However, you must sort out fact from fiction.

Thursday 24th

Today might be confusing or misleading. You may not be sure if the voice in your mind is your inner critic or cheerleader. Stop, slow down and find someone you trust implicitly to help you filter what you are feeling. This evening you may be more grounded and stable.

Friday 25th

Set your mind on your goals and today you can achieve something to be proud of. This may be a last-minute push to complete a long-standing project or a final decision about travel. Surprise yourself by taking the plunge and putting in more effort for this. Reward yourself in the evening doing something you love.

Saturday 26th

Green lights turn on everywhere you look today. Change is easy, your dreams are accessible, and by night you could feel like a person on a mission. You may be able to negotiate positive movement with your social groups from which all will benefit. Merging and connecting could be fruitful.

Sunday 27th

Mercury is now in your private sector. Here, he will pan for the gold you have hidden deep in your psyche. Don't be surprised if old habits or conditioning resurface to be healed. If you've been downplaying parts of yourself, now is the time to show them off.

Monday 28th

You may not be used to being humble, but that is how you might feel today. Your heart and actions are perfectly in sync as you walk your talk in the workplace. Elders or authority figures may show their appreciation for your efforts, and you could win some brownie points.

Tuesday 29th

Allow yourself to drift on a fluffy cloud. You deserve the rest and your imagination needs to be unleashed, if just for one day. You may desire to be alone, but you should also listen out for any useful tips and hints which come your way from your wider groups.

Wednesday 30th

Emotions may build and build today until you feel you could burst. Your inner compass is in your grasp and you may feel extremely optimistic about the future. Share the feeling with others as it could be infectious. You are on to a winner right now. Keep going.

Thursday 31st

Private time will help you to process new plans and ideas. When you are ready to initiate these, you will know. Just be careful not to take on too much and overload your time and energy. Make a schedule and review what is attainable and what is merely a pipe dream.

APRIL
. . . .

Friday 1st
Today's new moon will power you up to make positive goals and intentions regarding your most private life. This is a great time to think about old habits, conditioning and wounds that need clearing out or healing. Your mindset and energy to do this are in sync.

Saturday 2nd
You have plenty of support and encouragement from your social groups today. There might be a moment where you mourn a loss, but this is okay. Honour what it once meant to you. This evening you may be able to enjoy an evening doing what you love best and feeling good.

Sunday 3rd
If you listen very carefully to your inner voice, you may receive guidance on how to proceed with your inner work this year. Today could be a turning point on your road to becoming the best version of yourself. Exciting changes or new ideas can spur you on.

Monday 4th
Don't be put off with the heavy energy of the working week. Your outlook may be restricted, but this could only be that duty calls. Stick with it and get on with the tasks you've been given. This mood will pass. You are being asked to look at the bigger picture today.

Tuesday 5th

You may sense that something isn't right in the workplace. If you challenge this, you could come off worse. Concentrate on morals and responsibilities and put your energy into getting things done. Self-love is needed this evening. Don't beat yourself up for any perceived failures or shortcomings.

Wednesday 6th

Your busy mind recalls the good qualities you have which you tend to hide from others. Ask yourself why this is. Now is your time to show what you are made of. Shadow material from your psyche surfaces to urge you into the light. Make plans to bring your talents into the world.

Thursday 7th

An elder or good friend may be useful today as they will point out the good things about you. Let them be your cheerleader. You may desire to hold conversations with people who make you feel nurtured and safe now. Just don't let this go to your head. Be humble.

Friday 8th

There is great energy around today. You may have many thoughts and emotions which you easily communicate with loved ones. You could surprise yourself with how much this has lifted your spirits. Make sure it lasts and you don't fall back into old habits which stunted your progress.

Saturday 9th

You may feel like hiding away today. Perhaps your ego is giving you mixed messages. Do you want to shine or not? Connect to your dreams and inner compass. Allow your heart to fill with optimism and trust that this is right for you.

Sunday 10th

You could get itchy feet today. The satisfaction of being cared for is short-lived and you might wish to assert your independence once more. There could be a change which you are resisting. A trigger may have opened an old wound which stubbornly refuses to heal. Maybe you don't want to heal it.

Monday 11th

You may notice that you are called to speak up, agitate or reveal injustices in your social groups today. Make sure you get all your facts right before opening a can of worms. Alternatively, the planetary energy could bring you a way-marker for your personal path of self-development.

Tuesday 12th

You may be fired up today. This could manifest in ranting and raging or passionate, creative outbursts. Wanting your own way too much may cause friction. It's possible that an issue within your friendship groups is resolved or simply falls away into oblivion. Process this and fact-check every detail.

Wednesday 13th

You may feel at odds with yourself today. A desire for a break or retreat from daily life might attract you but could be an impossibility right now. You might feel temperamental and moody. It could, however, prompt you to be innovative and find a way to get-away whilst staying at home.

. . . .

Thursday 14th

Get creative or romantic today. You have a muse calling you
to manifest your longings but there may seem to be no time
in the day. Finish all your daily duties and put your remaining
energy into something for the greater good. Be expansive and
open-minded.

Friday 15th

Mars enters your social arena, so expect more energy here.
If there is a group venture which needs that extra push, you
will get it now. With four planets in this area, your social
and spiritual life could be chaotic or filled to the brim with
opportunities. Join in or miss out.

Saturday 16th

A full moon today could show where you have achieved
balance in your life. There may be some decision making still
to do, but you have the right energy to do this fairly. It may
involve a difficult change or ending, but if you see sense you
will do what is necessary.

Sunday 17th

An intense Moon amps up your relationships today. This
energy can make you extra seductive, but can also bring out
your dark shadows such as jealousy and manipulation. You
could be driven to get what you want at all costs. Think twice
if this is sneaky or underhand.

Monday 18th

A roller-coaster of energy makes for a tricky day. You may feel
self-righteous and could be sweet-talking a lover to get your own
way. This is likely to backfire on you and may reveal a side of you
which isn't nice. You may be justifying this to yourself by evening.

Tuesday 19th

You may wish to run away today, but this could be because you don't know how to remedy recent problems. If escaping is your default action to trouble, you will only make things worse. Cut your losses and eat humble pie as this will enhance your path of self-development.

Wednesday 20th

The Sun enters your sign today. Happy birthday! A yearning to explore the wider world may fill you. You may realise that this is an avoidance tactic you might use when refusing to do your inner work. Friends might annoy you now and leave you little time for daydreaming alone.

Thursday 21st

You may find a way to satisfy your travel urges today. This may be in the form of higher learning or connecting with people outside your community. Something may come up at work which helps you to make a slow but steady plan. Social groups could have invitations for you.

Friday 22nd

You may have some fabulous ideas today if you can think outside the box. Processing these when alone can give you food for thought and get you back on track with your own desires and wishes. If you really want to grow into your best self, listen to your innermost voice.

Saturday 23rd

A shift in your focus comes naturally now. It may be that you've let an idea or unachievable plan go. This will open up new space for you to plant the right seeds. Try not to be too stubborn today and listen to any advice you are given.

Sunday 24th

You may wake to feel agitated. This could be your impatience looking for an outlet or immediate release. Think of something you enjoy but is hard to begin. Once you've started, you may be glad you did so. Watch what you say with elders or authority figures. Be responsible and kind.

Monday 25th

That restless feeling lingers, but this is temporary. Try to be productive today as this will help. Friends can also be useful now as you need to connect and merge with like-minded others. This gives you a better perspective of yourself and your natural responses. Self-care will ease your mind.

Tuesday 26th

Get ready for action today. You could be in the mood for a meaningful connection with someone special. You may have your desires met today in unusual ways. Consider activities which are energetic and require problem-solving as these will lift your mood greatly. You win when you do a job well.

Wednesday 27th

This is a day for love and romance. Your wider friendship circles may provide you with a new love interest and make your heart race. This could also be an event or cause which stimulates your senses and makes you feel at one with the world outside your window.

Thursday 28th

Listen to your own heart and you may see where change
is not only necessary but desired. You can pave the way for
good things to come in if you can leave old things behind.
This could be the beginning of a slow-growing seed which
can be nurtured into a fine flower.

Friday 29th

Pluto turns retrograde today. This might slow down change
for you to reassess its value. You may have a period of months
where transformation rather than complete change happens.
Take care of your responsibilities within social groups today.
Your role is important to the whole.

Saturday 30th

A new moon in your sign is an excellent opportunity to make
goals and intentions regarding how you are viewed. You may
have started to see a new you and wish to present it to the
outside world. This Moon comes with a solar eclipse, so expect
a wild card which opens a window.

MAY

. . . .

Sunday 1st

Today you have the right amount of energy to make positive
changes which will benefit your groups. You may have
seen something in a different light and now feel far more
compassion than you previously did. Aim for sensual pleasures
to help you wind down this evening.

Monday 2nd

Happiness may spill from you today and you could be chatting
or even singing through your day. Your heart and mind are in
sync and you feel balanced. Venus dips into your most private
zone and will give you the courage you need to tackle old
wounds and excavate the gold hidden in your psyche.

Tuesday 3rd

Frustration may get the better of you today. Remember that
this reminds you to get grounded and do something practical.
This isn't difficult for a Taurus, as you cope better than most
with staying put. It may just be that messages or money
matters aren't clear right now.

Wednesday 4th

If it feels that you're way off the mark today, try connecting
with your wider groups and brainstorming ideas. It's possible
to have a momentous breakthrough which can be spiritual or
new knowledge which you could fully embrace. If you need to
break free, do it today.

Thursday 5th

Sparks may fly as your mind churns out idea after idea. Alternatively, your emotions could be close to the edge and ready to erupt. It's possible that a trigger from the past has resurfaced and you may be a raging bull today. You may be extra protective and defensive.

Friday 6th

Soothing words of self-love are important and helpful now. You may find that staying in the comfort of your own home is a safety net. Surround yourself with what you love and give yourself permission to have feelings. This is all part of the healing process, so try not to push it away.

Saturday 7th

You may feel a surge of love and optimism as you connect with like-minded people. The energy is good for showing yourself in your best light. What can you learn from the universe or from your interest groups today? There may be something which spurs you on to keep growing.

Sunday 8th

Take a day of being good to yourself and notice how you rarely do this. It may feel unnatural but will do you the world of good. By evening you may feel restless and need to let off steam. Don't be tempted to jump online, go outside or do some exercise.

Monday 9th

The week may begin with a few setbacks that you need to attend to. This could spoil your mood and make you grumble or complain. It would be a good idea to get ready for the next Mercury retrograde which starts tomorrow. Back up devices and tie up loose ends.

Tuesday 10th

Mercury may play tricks with your money this time around. You may want to check your bank balance for any outstanding payments. Check every detail and be methodical today and it will pay off. Ensure that decisions and conversations are clear and don't sign any contracts just yet.

Wednesday 11th

Jupiter bounces into your most private thoughts. This will bring more optimism and fairness to your thought processes. You may wish to be creative but can't get motivated although you have plenty of fresh ideas to implement. Let this pass and stick to something you've already been working on.

Thursday 12th

Duty calls you today. You may need to find a good balance between home and work and ensure you have time left for fun. Making decisions may be easier if you remember that Mercury needs you to clarify everything. If you need to ask for help or unbiased advice, do it.

Friday 13th

You may not feel loveable this morning and could be reprimanding yourself for old mistakes. Learn to forgive yourself for these. This is a good day for making a long-term plan for getting what you want from life. The future beckons and you get a glimpse of your role in it.

Saturday 14th

If you're grieving over a small loss, allow yourself to feel those emotions. Your shadow side could make an appearance and you may want to hide it. Alternatively, you have an opportunity to put a lot of energy into righting a wrong and moving on from a particular phase.

Sunday 15th

You'll likely feel exposed and irritable today. However, this energy can be used positively and can guide you to what you want through knowing exactly what you don't want. Try not to get caught up in ego clashes with authority figures. Keep within healthy boundaries.

Monday 16th

A full moon with a lunar eclipse may close a window on your relationship issues. This wild card could let your shadow trick you and you may have intense feelings which trouble you. Emotions may be up and down today. Make sure that communications are clear if speaking from the heart.

Tuesday 17th

Today you may be prepared to go as deep and as far as you need to. This will probably involve your private life or the most intimate side of a relationship. You need not fear the unknown as you are willing to face it head-on. Have compassion for self and others.

Wednesday 18th

A kick-start helps to get you moving today. There could be something which is totally aligned to your purpose and truth and you must grab it now or risk losing it. It's natural to feel some anticipation, but you must trust that this is right for you and accept it.

. . . .

Thursday 19th

An increasing doubt may creep into your awareness.
This is meant to test and see if you fall back into your default
behaviours. Keep moving forward one step at a time and you
may surprise yourself today. Don't listen to your inner critic
as it will pull you off course.

Friday 20th

You're a fighter this morning and nothing can stop you
with your goals. You may be emotionally attached to events
which make the day go without a hitch. Speak your truth
and you won't go wrong. Even Mercury is on your side today.
Conversations are easier and have more quality.

Saturday 21st

Your job is to listen to everything today. Messages, dream
symbols and advice could lead you on a process which may
change a few things at work. You may need to put others first
and let go of a few items from your own agenda. Be selfless now.

Sunday 22nd

This can be a tricky day where you might need to sort through
new information and use it wisely. Your wider friendship
groups may be experiencing upheaval or disconnect. If you
aren't directly involved, stay out of it. Return when all is calm,
and you can exercise reason.

Monday 23rd

Mercury slips back into your sign. Be mindful that this may
mean unintentional slip-ups and accidents. Is there something
you need to put extra effort into? This could be regarding
spiritual practice, interest groups or your dreams. Give it one
last push now and you may find something to be pleased about.

Tuesday 24th

You feel close to your inner compass today but may need confirmation from another source. If you can see that you need to work for what you want, all will be well. If you think it will come to you as if by magic, you will be disappointed.

Wednesday 25th

Egos and emotions could be huge and exaggerated. Your inner world could be supporting this but may also lead to a false sense of security. A word from a wise person could plant seeds in your soul which you can be nurtured into something beautiful. Watch out for illusions before bedtime.

Thursday 26th

Older people are helping you. It may be that you have more or new responsibility and you're enjoying it. Today you may be rooting for the underdog and helping towards a good cause. You may find that this also helps to heal something from within your psyche.

Friday 27th

Compassion for yourself might fill you today, but this comes with a cost. You may need to make a small sacrifice in order to finally heal an old wound or do the right thing today. Put yourself out there and let others see how hard you're working at this.

Saturday 28th

You may experience a few tremors as something is shifting. These don't have to develop into an eruption, but they could show you new paths which were once hidden. Your ruler Venus comes home to your sign. Expect more self-love, quality, beauty and even money to come in for you now.

Sunday 29th

Be very careful what you say today. The potential is there for you to stir up some trouble or say something you shouldn't. Tempers may be larger than usual and be close to the edge. You can save yourself by using this energy at the gym or by decluttering.

Monday 30th

A new moon gives you the chance to make plans to enhance your surroundings and love life. You may have a few decisions to make now, but these could be as simple as choosing wallpaper or a new look for yourself. They could also be irreversible, so choose wisely.

Tuesday 31st

You may need advice on something which is overwhelming you. This could be something in your thought processes or habits. Work issues could also be playing on your mind. This may not leave any time for dreaming and may not resonate with your personal truth. Get your head down and do what's necessary.

JUNE

. . . .

Wednesday 1st

Today you wish to be nourished by good conversations. Your
siblings may give you the boost you require. Your inner work
might be too much today, and you may like to switch off and
have some family fun instead. Feed your soul with whatever
makes you feel safe and secure. Let your inner child play.

Thursday 2nd

Breaking free from expectations excites you today. You
may notice that some people still think of you as you were
a long time ago. Prove to them how much you've grown.
Alternatively, you may do something out of the ordinary just
for the hell of it.

Friday 3rd

Mercury turns direct and you may now think about
committing to long-term-projects. Let your imagination free
and find something which is more in tune with the new you
and who you wish to be. Self-expression will be easy in the next
few days. Don't let others take control of your plans.

Saturday 4th

Saturn turns retrograde now. He is the biggest teacher of the
planets. You may learn how to do something differently at
work. This will require that you know your boundaries and
those of others. There is still a lot to be excavated in your
psyche, but take it slowly.

Sunday 5th

Today may be very frustrating. You may be wanting your own way too much and causing unnecessary tension. Blocks and restrictions show you that this is non-negotiable, so give up before you have a mini tantrum. Find a workaround solution which is safe and responsible. Let your actions match your words.

Monday 6th

Your head and heart aren't in sync and you may find that whatever you say just doesn't feel right for you. You may need to consider what your role is in a relationship. If this is a romance, it needs to be unconditional or it won't work. Check in with your health today.

Tuesday 7th

This is a good day to start something new concerning your physical body. An exercise regime or healthy eating plan would be good. New and innovative ways of looking after yourself will make you glow, and others will be wondering how you did it. Do what you can to help others.

Wednesday 8th

Your inner compass seems to be evading you, but if you stand still and look hard enough, you'll see it's still there. Maybe now is not the time to do anything about it. Grounding energy can help you to get on with practical things today and this suits you.

Thursday 9th

Others may require too much of your attention. Be careful as this may be draining, and you will need to detach somehow. It could be that you are not finding the time to work on your own plans for self-development but helping others in need. Fill your own cup first.

Friday 10th

A lesson about boundaries may present itself. There could be a change or ending which you need to make. Relationships are the focus for the weekend, and you could be in for an intense couple of days. Be mindful not to project your unwanted baggage onto those you love.

Saturday 11th

You may be working up to a blow-out of some kind. This could be a delicious and seductive time with a partner, but may also be a row. There is an element of selfishness within you and an appetite which needs satisfying. How you manage this is up to you.

Sunday 12th

The tension rises and your close personal relationships will feel it the most. You need to be mindful of crossing borders uninvited. If you are thinking about past relationships, this will only end in tears. Your head and heart are not aligned, and you may risk a significant upset.

Monday 13th

Learning how to converse with a loved one may rescue your relationship. Perhaps you need to open up more and let them into your deepest and most private thoughts. They may surprise you by knowing how to respond and treat you in the way you wish to be treated.

Tuesday 14th

A full moon lights up your feelings of connecting to places far and wide. You may be learning a new philosophy or religion. This could make a deep impact on your soul and you may yearn for foreign travel. Exploring the depths of your own environment and relationships must come first.

Wednesday 15th

You may be looking at a virtual mountain top and getting overwhelmed. Visualise yourself at the summit, and with the Taurus inclination to be determined and steadfast, you will know that this climb is possible. However, if this includes your inner work, it could be daunting too.

Thursday 16th

There is enough earth energy for you to secure your footing and get through your day. Your ruler Venus is calling you and acting as your cheerleader now. She can help you attract love, harmony and money, so use this energy and do something practical to make sure these come your way.

Friday 17th

You may be more outgoing and focused than usual. Good things are on the agenda for today, so stay alert to any possibilities. At work, you may find that you are noticed for doing a job well. This can give you an optimistic outlook ready for the weekend.

Saturday 18th

A challenging day may stop you in your tracks and result in you doing nothing. You don't need to be productive today, but what will benefit is pausing and assessing your path so far. Take a rest stop and evaluate where you are and how you got there. Then proceed.

Sunday 19th

An invitation from friends or spiritual groups can help to ease your tension. Although you may not be thinking straight, you might benefit from seeing a different perspective. Allow your concerns to dissolve and make you fresh for the coming week. Don't let busy thoughts bother you. Just relax.

Monday 20th

You may surprise yourself today. It's possible that you've found a softer approach to a task that has been bothering you. As you reattach to your inner compass, take some time to look at the view and make sure it's still right for you. Have that conversation you've been avoiding.

Tuesday 21st

The summer solstice invites you to enjoy the longest day. The planetary energy suggests that you may be happy turning inward and finding the golden nuggets hidden in your psyche. You may have more success with this today as you may feel safer and protected by maternal strength. Turn to female relatives for support.

Wednesday 22nd

In direct contrast to yesterday, this may be a day of action. It could also be a time where your private thoughts get disturbed. You may be more driven to explore the triggers, or you may still be too emotionally attached to discern right action. If in doubt, do nothing.

Thursday 23rd

Venus enters an area which determines how you attract quality and what you value most. You may now find that decisions concerning love come easier. You may have more than one option to choose from, but after careful consideration, you will make your decision. It will feel right.

Friday 24th

Today can be restless, temperamental or mind-blowing. This can be both good and bad. If you act wisely and seek pleasure rather than pain, you may have an enjoyable day. If, however, you choose to pick faults then a tumultuous day awaits you. You could also rebel against restraint now.

Saturday 25th

You may have a dreamy day where you reap what you have recently sown. Look out for a signpost which entices you towards a future you may love. Completions and transformations can be done without the usual angst today. This could open up new space for your personal growth.

Sunday 26th

There is lovely energy available to you now. Conversations can be stimulating, and you have a special someone who knows just what to say to you. You may get lost in a fantasy land or be seduced by your wildest fantasies. Keep one foot on the ground.

Monday 27th

Your mood may continue to match your mind right now. Thoughts will need to be filtered through your heart before processed. A keen drive to look at your inner work can make you more respectful of other's boundaries as you are recognising your own.

Tuesday 28th

Neptune, your inner compass turns retrograde today. This may cause some confusion within your social groups. It may also be a time when liars and cheats are exposed. Use this as a rest stop and gather your resources and allies ready for when the journey continues. You may feel a little vulnerable today.

Wednesday 29th

A new moon in your communication area may be what you
need to open up to a different level with someone. This might be
something that is needed in your family. It may also be a time
to protect the weak or discuss new tactics concerning security.

Thursday 30th

Expect the unexpected today and you won't be disappointed.
You may get a hint of something untoward in your social
groups. This will likely come undone in the coming months.
Stay out of power struggles and control issues. Be the
protector and keep yourself and loved ones safe.

JULY

· · · · · · · · · · · · · · · · · · ·

Friday 1st

You may wish to assert your independence and have your say today. A piece of your psyche surfaces for healing and you may deal with it well. In fact, you may be so pleased with yourself that by evening you are looking for a little recognition or reward. Treat yourself to something nice.

Saturday 2nd

This can be a challenging day and you will need to take stock of a few things. It may be money problems which need sorting. Look for finances you share with another and subscriptions you could cancel. You may feel financially unable to go ahead with some of your plans.

Sunday 3rd

Family can be a cause of tension, especially elders or people you must listen to. Your inner child may have a few tantrums. You have a chance to talk about this and put your point of view across. Allow good advice to be integrated rather than push it away through stubbornness.

Monday 4th

Don't feel hurried into dealing with a deeply held issue. There may be something you can do about it now, but you could also have more triggers to deal with. You may find that you are doing more for others than for yourself today and this doesn't help your mood.

Tuesday 5th

Mars enters your sign. This could make you more determined and argumentative. However, it could also be the push you need to present yourself as ready and willing. Communications become more caring and you can negotiate in a loving, protective manner. Do something like exercise this evening. Get grounded.

Wednesday 6th

It may be tricky to find a good balance of everyday duties and private time. Inner problems seem bigger and you may wish to escape and deal with them. Try to communicate this to people who are relying on you and you may find that they are sympathetic.

Thursday 7th

Today you may be more willing to take care of the small details as you can see how they will benefit you. Finances might improve if you can listen to good advice. There may be a blockage or restriction in the workplace, but this serves to help you find a better way.

Friday 8th

One to one relationships need your attention now. You may have intense feelings which you can communicate with love. However, this may leave you feeling conflicted or vulnerable. Are you getting what you need or just looking for what you want from your love relationships? Compromise is necessary.

Saturday 9th

Old feelings and experiences may dampen your mood. You could be using these as excuses for not relating in a respectful and considerate manner. The energy suggests that you should forget the past and move on. Tension could build and get out of hand. Be ready for the fallout.

Sunday 10th

You can be more outgoing today, but this may be a disguise. It's possible that you wish to run away, mentally or physically. Consider whether you or not you are thriving on tension which may be acting as a trigger for action. It may also be a coping mechanism you use for avoidance.

Monday 11th

Be careful about your spending today. You may be making purchases to soothe yourself, but these could also cause you further stress if they are short-term fixes. A yearning to get away could overpower you this evening. Try thinking about booking a break which feeds your soul and lifts your spirits.

Tuesday 12th

You may be more likely to settle into the working week now. Ideas may have been ruminating in your mind and it's possible to implement one or two. You have the right energy to make these happen albeit with slow and steady care. No rushing required, take one step at a time.

Wednesday 13th

A full moon may mean that you have completed a long-standing project. This can be most satisfying but may have you wondering what's next. Your social status may have reached a level you are happy with, but don't get big-headed. Boasting won't do you any favours.

Thursday 14th

Agitation can make you impulsive and without thinking, you may make a big change. Think twice before acting on impulse or misinformation as you could come away from this looking foolish. However, this energy may also mean that you are acting for the greater good and putting your own needs last.

Friday 15th

You may be acting out of character or trying to push against the norm today. Take time to pause and think about what you are doing. If you still feel justified, consider the consequences. There may be more than you involved. Take advice from someone with more experience.

Saturday 16th

Friendship and interest groups may fill your time this weekend. You could be feeling extra sociable and wish to spend quality time with close friends. It could be that a friend needs you to listen to them and your role is to offer compassion and support. This can do you both good.

Sunday 17th

Today you may find someone with whom you can share your dreams. Someone may surprise you with their existing knowledge and passion for the same ideals. This would be a good time to make a connection which is based on mutual interests and quality conversations. Don't miss this opportunity.

Monday 18th

You enter a period where communications are flavoured with beauty and compassion. A soul friend may come into your awareness. You may notice that you are more inspired to look for experiences and connections that have more value. This could touch you deeply and you will need to process your feelings.

Tuesday 19th

Your heart could swell today. You may have been given a boost of pure joy and optimism recently. A shift in your thinking takes you to a place where you are more likely to speak your truth and be honest about what you want. Family may be shocked or supportive now.

Wednesday 20th

From where you are standing, some changes don't look so bad. They may be more of an adjustment than a permanent change. You feel you can handle this. It may mean that you give up a few things which haven't been working for you, but you accept this with grace.

Thursday 21st

The Moon in your sign gives you added emotional strength.
Stop worrying about how you appear to others. Instead,
concentrate on your own divine essence and being true to
that. You could be feeling assertive today and initiate a small
project. You may also desire romantic and sensual company.

Friday 22nd

You have stirrings in your gut which are telling you
something. It may be that you want to break free from the
norm. It could also be a deeply earth moving revelation. Your
dreams are in sight and it's time to reach out and grab them.
Let your inner child free.

Saturday 23rd

If you have decisions to make today, keep them light-hearted
and playful. Whatever you decide will make you happy. There is
a lot to be thankful for now. It's easy for you to communicate
your most private thoughts and this pleases you greatly. You
have a renewed passion for life.

Sunday 24th

Finances and equality may get a boost today. This is a day with
joyful planetary energy. Use it wisely or lose the opportunity
to bounce around like a child. You may be as unfiltered as you
wish, and this could bring you a day filled with laughter.

Monday 25th

You may come back down to the daily grind with a bump
today. Don't worry too much if you feel grumpy about it,
this is natural after such a high. You may resent not having
time to pursue your new passions, but will enjoy meaningful
conversations after the work is done.

Tuesday 26th

Stick to the tasks you've been given today and keep your head down. You may have another chance this evening to wallow in self-care or the loving touch of someone special. These may be simple chat messages but could light your darkest corners. One warning: don't make it all about you.

Wednesday 27th

You have the right energy to power through your day easily. You are driven and excited enough to keep the momentum from becoming dull. Inject a little of this into your own dreams this evening, even if it is simply telling a close friend or sibling your deepest wishes.

Thursday 28th

A Moon full of passion allows you to set goals and intentions regarding truly being your best self. Surprise yourself and make a vision board. Jupiter turns retrograde today, so you may find that this becomes a period of re-evaluating big plans and making them smaller and more easily attainable.

Friday 29th

Today may be challenging and feel like a backward step. Stick with it as this energy is temporary and will pass. If you feel irritable and need to let off some excess energy then you would be better off doing physical exercise, getting out in nature or cooking something delicious for yourself.

Saturday 30th

Your heart and head are in sync. However, this could mean that you say what you feel to the wrong people. Not everyone will be open to your ideas today and you could clash with a leader or teacher. Perhaps you overstep the mark and get put in your place.

Sunday 31st

Your mouth could run away with you today. Are you perpetuating an argument because you want to be proved right? This is the proverbial bull in the china shop energy, so if you persist, you may see a lot crashing down all around you. Guess who will be picking up the pieces.

AUGUST
. . . .

Monday 1st
Highly sexual, sensual and volatile energy is in your sign.
You may choose to use this for your own benefit. It could also
imply that a volcanic eruption is about to blow up in your face.
It will also give you a signpost with a definite message.

Tuesday 2nd
Today is still pretty unstable. You may experience mind-
blowing revelations which rock your world. Come evening,
you may be trying to process this but not making sense of it.
Perhaps this is a cue to feel the feelings and go with them.
You may be in for a few surprises.

Wednesday 3rd
The planetary energy turns romantic and you may settle
down into a more mundane but no less sensual way of
communicating with a loved one. You may both be depleted
and need to rest. Take care of your health now and understand
that what makes you tick, doesn't necessarily heal.

Thursday 4th
Relationships remain in focus but with an edge of mystery. It
might be the right time to discuss your roles and expectations.
Boundaries become important now but may get lost as you
merge into a state of unconditional behaviour. Talks may be
intense and a little taboo.

Friday 5th

Try not to judge a lover by your experience of the past.
You may notice that you are still being triggered by
past relationships and wish for this not to impact a new
relationship or level of relating. If you are feeling restless,
try not to project that tension outwards.

Saturday 6th

A lot of watery, emotional energy may make you feel lost or
ungrounded. If you aren't used to this overflow, look for your
inner compass and hold tight. It may be a case of learning
to go with the flow or missing out on deep connections with
someone you admire.

Sunday 7th

You may struggle to find the rationale for the way you feel
right now. Don't bother trying as it will continue to be
inaccessible. This is a lesson in relating with feelings and not
practical things. You must learn to trust now. Your shadow
may cause you some problems if you act out.

Monday 8th

As much as you would like to break free and broaden your
horizons, you might be finding that once again, this is an escape
route you use too often. By evening you may be happier and find
your footing again. This time you will be surer of your path ahead.

Tuesday 9th

Good, solid, practical energy gives you something to hold on
to. Take some time to look at the view from where you are
standing. Is the summit worth the climb or would you prefer
to retreat and walk on familiar territory? Adventure calls if
you're willing to listen.

Wednesday 10th

Something has piqued your interest and you have the motivation and desire to move on up. You may realise that you're being asked to make a change, and this frightens you. When you've had time to think, you will understand that this is probably the best move of the year.

Thursday 11th

Take some time to consider how you are presenting yourself right now. Are you really being true to yourself or do you still wear a mask? Venus shifts signs and becomes the compassionate female warrior to help you stay fixed on expressing your truth and walking your talk.

Friday 12th

Today's full moon may highlight a culmination of projects related to travel and your wider communities. You may see that some things didn't work quite as planned. Pause and reflect before taking any action on this. Reassess your personal boundaries and ensure they are healthy and strong.

Saturday 13th

You may wish to be alone today. Your mind may be muddled, and you could be too subjective to work a problem through. A spiritual practice may help to clear your mind. Connect to the divine and get centred. Merging with something bigger than yourself may help to clarify your thoughts.

Sunday 14th

As you come up next to your inner compass you may see what is holding you back. With a gentle push, remove these things from your life with love. A little exertion may be enough to clear some space in your heart and mind. Don't be too eager to fill it up again yet.

Monday 15th

Rooting around in your psyche, you may unearth a few secret desires which have yet to be fulfilled. Bring them out into the open and add them to your vision board. They may be as simple as catching up with people or a special treat for yourself.

Tuesday 16th

Fiery energy helps you to move through your day with great passion. You may be able to find unique solutions to problems or enhance your love life with stimulating conversation which is good for your soul. If something doesn't feel right by evening, it could just be a yearning for a holiday.

Wednesday 17th

The Moon dips into your sign but may make you tired or unwilling to engage today. You might not feel like being outspoken and speaking your truth now. This phase will pass, so while you are feeling it, take time out and be good to yourself. Try not to argue with loved ones.

Thursday 18th

You are unable to stay down for long as restless energy fill you with a need to move. There may be something regarding finances or values which needs to be completed now. A last-minute push may give you more incentive and leave you with a clear mind.

Friday 19th

That familiar urge to change everything around you could threaten to overwhelm you now. You may wish to do some DIY and switch up your immediate environment or make a change to your appearance. Think of a way to beautify what you see every day as this could lift your spirits.

Saturday 20th

A weekend of conversation or learning something new may be good. There may be a way to combine this with what brings you pleasure. Messages can bring you joy and get you wondering. If you can see value in this, keep doing it. Your love life will benefit too.

Sunday 21st

This may be a challenging day where the pleasures that you seek are unavailable or just not right for you. Don't try to mould them into alignment as they could taint your personal dreams and be hard to get rid of. Refrain from short-term gains today.

Monday 22nd

Say what you mean today. If something comes across as superficial, you may be judged later. You may need to feel more secure and gather trusted resources around you. Triggers affecting your old grudges might surface to be healed. Flush them out of your system now.

Tuesday 23rd

The Sun enters your creative and romantic zone. You may also need to check in with your health now, but it may also be on top form during the Sun's visit. Eating a favourite meal can bring back memories which can delight you. You might be surprised by how much you miss someone.

Wednesday 24th

Uranus turns retrograde in your sign. This may signal a period where you are more stubborn and refuse to try anything new. If you are feeling restricted or smothered, wait until this afternoon when the energy suggests that you have more freedom of speech and can be yourself.

Thursday 25th

Emotions may feel stuck today. Although you feel that you are genuinely trying your best to truthful and upfront, it may be that you have hit a sore spot with another person and this needs to be healed. If you can't help them, give them the space they need.

Friday 26th

Your negotiating skills may be called upon over the next few weeks. You might have hit a glitch in your romance and need to find an appropriate compromise. Heavy energy may weigh upon you and restrict your ability to reach out and connect in a way which benefits all.

Saturday 27th

It's likely that you feel drained now and this may lead you to feel hopeless. This will pass, so use the new moon to look at your health goals and any creative or romantic pursuits. Planning and scheduling may take your mood to a different level and dissipate any gloominess.

Sunday 28th

Family issues may cause stress today as it's possible that your agenda clashes with an elder. Don't try breaching boundaries to get at someone who doesn't want to be approached. If you are patient, this may be achieved by being respectful and accept the fact that you can be too pushy sometimes.

Monday 29th

Balance is more achievable now as your head and heart are in sync. You may get a boost from thinking logically and rationally about a situation. This may enable you to proceed, make amends and find a workable solution for all. Others need you to be adaptable now.

Tuesday 30th

Retreat is your best tactic today. There is a battle between what you want and what others want, and you may not be able to reconcile it without tension. Evaluating everything may make you more muddled and this won't help anyone. If you see unfairness, stay alert and raise it when appropriate.

Wednesday 31st

Pushing against the flow will be of no help today. You may have intense feelings of jealousy as your shadow comes out to play. If you find that you're projecting, withdraw and have some alone time. Alternatively, a partner may come to the rescue, but you must listen to what they say.

SEPTEMBER

. . . .

Thursday 1st

Your love life may enjoy some action or a decluttering of toxic emotions. It may be the time to put all cards on the table and discuss tricky issues which are not conducive to your relationship. Clear the air and let the baggage go. Don't allow the past to influence the present.

Friday 2nd

It may be difficult to deal with deeply felt emotions that come up. You may feel like rebelling or struggling with new restrictions on your freedom. Reaching out to your inner compass can help steady you and allow you to see that change is a necessary part of growth.

Saturday 3rd

You could still be challenged by negative thoughts swimming around in your psyche. These aren't healthy and a detox of your soul may be needed. Resist the urge to run away and not deal with these troubles. Find your centre of calm and explore all your options before making decisions.

Sunday 4th

An understanding may be reached as you are in the right frame of mind to listen. Boundaries can be respected and worked with. You may consider stretching some and retracting others. There may be borders that dissolve without you needing to do anything. Venus asks you to keep an open heart today.

Monday 5th

Your ruler, Venus shifts into your romantic and creative zone. What beauty and harmony could you create now? Love affairs are highlighted, and you may find your muse. You may still need to expand your mind when relating and this could be challenging today. Go easy on yourself.

Tuesday 6th

There is much nicer energy for you now. You may be able to fill that urge to travel, explore and dream in a healthy way. Making grounded plans and committing to them is a good start. This may be a long-term project but will give you something to look forward to.

Wednesday 7th

You continue to be outgoing and this shows in the workplace. You may be successful at overcoming obstacles simply by taking a leap of faith. This evening your mind and energy are geared towards having quality discussions. Passionate discourses are possible, and these may energise you enough to want more.

Thursday 8th

Today you may be throwing your hands up in the air as you spot more challenges in your way. You are likely to be difficult to deal with. Stop and look at what is blocking you. Ask yourself why? Then ask yourself if the way you are reacting to this is healthy.

Friday 9th

You may have a need for your friends today. If your creative side is lacking in inspiration, turn to your social groups and notice how you merge and connect. Individuality within a group is important and this is the time to show that you appreciate other's uniqueness too.

Saturday 10th

Mercury turns retrograde today. This will mainly affect your mundane duties and health. It will be a time to clear out and make things easier. A full moon also lights up your social and interest groups and later connects to your inner compass. There is a lot to process today.

Sunday 11th

Take a day off and hide under the duvet. You could be feeling attacked or hopeless. This phase will pass but, in the meantime, you may wish to do some quiet inner work. Try making small intentions or look at what you wish to change during Mercury retrograde.

Monday 12th

Your energy returns and you may be able to sustain it long enough to get through your day. If you feel stuck by evening, don't push anything. Step back and give yourself enough space to unwind. It may be a problem that can wait until tomorrow or a person who is causing tension.

Tuesday 13th

You can be your best self today and display all those Taurean qualities of being slow, dependable and resourceful. As you plod through the day, notice the quality and harmony you bring when you are on top form. Keep that vibe going for as long as you can.

Wednesday 14th

This is a good day for a detox or a special self-care routine. You may think about switching things up and redecorating your home. It may also be your appearance you would like to change. If you make a permanent change, don't be too outrageous or you might regret it.

Thursday 15th

Try looking at something from a different perspective today. You may see your inner compass and watch some of your hopes and dreams disappear. Remember to assess whether they are truly in line with your needs. This may be the detox you need to move on with a lighter load.

Friday 16th

Take care of your resources today. You may be spending too much or using up your brain space on something which isn't worthy. A struggle with balancing all your tasks is possible and you may feel resentful. By evening you should relax as you may be totally drained.

Saturday 17th

Tricky energy asks you to consider how you may be overloaded doing things for others. There may also be a financial issue which needs attention. Friendships can be more of a hindrance now as your personal agenda may clash with that of the collective. Have your interactions lost the quality you seek?

Sunday 18th

Your best bet now is to seek solace with those who know you best. Recreating an environment in which you feel nurtured and safe would be good for you. Be mindful of your talk as gossip is rife and could get out of hand. Be fair and take time to process.

Monday 19th

The energy picks up and lets you see that when something unsavoury surfaces, it's asking to be healed. You may not notice this immediately, but with more agitation, you might see it in a different light. From your safety net, it may not look as bad as you first thought.

Tuesday 20th

A happier mood brings a lighter step today. A little disturbance in your love life may lead to a new level of understanding. You may also have found a breakthrough in a creative project. Protecting and defending may meet in the middle and join forces.

Wednesday 21st

You could be prone to saying too much and being brutally honest today. Speak your truth by all means but pause first. Ask yourself whether what you are saying is kind, true and respectful. It may hit a sore spot deep inside you and you could end up causing yourself some harm too.

Thursday 22nd

Be careful of overdoing things today. You may wake and begin the day as if you are on a mission, but you may tire easily. This is another day where you must not push boundaries. Your own or other people's. Use your energy to find solutions and learn something new.

Friday 23rd

The Sun enters your health and duties area. It's especially important that you listen to your body's needs now. What can you do to lessen your duties and obligations and make more time for yourself? Mercury may stir up trouble in your love life now. Make all communication noticeably clear.

Saturday 24th

Friends and lovers both need your attention. It may not be possible to please all. You might also find that something is conflicting with your innermost dreams. Do you feel off-balance? How can you work around this without draining yourself? Solutions may come to you by evening.

Sunday 25th

You may feel selfish today as you need to take care of your own needs. This is self-care and is not at all selfish. It's likely that you simply can't communicate this effectively to others. A new moon helps you to redress the balance between relating and doing things for yourself.

Monday 26th

Your ruler, Venus, needs you to listen today. Have a talk with your inner child and ask if there's anything you could be doing to add more love and laughter to your life. You may wish to play or create something from this. Use the day to get artistic and use it as therapy.

Tuesday 27th

Watch out for Mercury's tricks today. You may see something cleaned out of your life and be relieved. However, this could return. Perhaps it's not meant to leave but to be transformed somehow. Wait a week or so before making anything permanent. Don't dispose of anything just yet.

Wednesday 28th

Partner time is highlighted now. You may desire the intense pleasure of someone's company. This may also give your shadow a chance to come out and play. Be warned that unhealthy shadow material is what you project, but your partner could bring out the golden shadow which you keep hidden from most people.

Thursday 29th

You may be thinking of the past, especially concerning relationships or other such joint ventures. If something crops up which you don't like, deal with it then throw it in the cosmic waste bin. Relating should be a little easier and healthier as you may work as a couple more productively.

Friday 30th

Today you have a chance to reach a new level in your love relationship. Intimacy may be deeper and suit both. You could be exploring new territory together or literally planning a trip or new study. You may be interested in the wider world and its religions or philosophies.

OCTOBER

· · · · · · · · · · · · · · · · · ·

Saturday 1st

The planetary energy is pretty heavy today. What begins as
a day with unhelpful restrictions could become a day when
you wish you had never got up. You can't do anything right
today. Spend quality time at home with a few good travel
documentaries and mentally plan your next trip.

Sunday 2nd

Mercury turns direct today and as if by magic you may see
mists fall away and reveal a truth which has been hidden. This
may be within your love life or your friends' circle. You may
have a heavy heart as you take baby steps to process what this
means for you.

Monday 3rd

Draw in useful skills you learned in the past and use them
again. If added to your current workload they may make you
more efficient and productive. You could realise the value of
going slowly with certain projects and apply these old skills in
a truly innovative way.

Tuesday 4th

As the energy shifts, you seek more connection with others.
That may be business meetings or social networking with like-
minded people. You may meet someone new who can support
any inner work you now need to do. However, scrutinise them
and check their credentials. Then give them a fair chance.

Wednesday 5th

It may take you all day to pick up the pace. The problem is that you may feel stuck and reluctant to move in the wrong way. You may end up having to take a leap of faith and running right into a boundary problem. Mental activity is high but confusing.

Thursday 6th

Today, your interest groups may provide the stimulation you need. It may feel a little like you're swimming alone in a big ocean until you meet your tribe. This can provoke emotions from deep inside which can surface and have you asking big questions such as "where do I belong?"

Friday 7th

Good grounding energy gives you a life jacket to help you keep afloat. You may get too used to this ethereal energy and drift far away, but your inner voice tells you to go back to the shore. Once there, you may do some rational and practical thinking which suits you.

Saturday 8th

You catch sight of your true north, your inner compass. This may be your saving grace today which pulls you back to the earthly plane. If you have a muddled mind, go with your heart. This evening you are more inspired to think about what needs to be put right.

Sunday 9th

Pluto turns direct and leads you to a full moon which lights up the darkest corners of your psyche. You may have a startling realisation of what needs to change. You may let go of something you have been holding on to for too long. This may include a romance.

Monday 10th

Schedule a health check-up and get in touch with people you have neglected recently. Decisions regarding your resources may be made easier today if you take time to process what you need and what has been holding you back. End the day by doing something you love.

Tuesday 11th

Negotiations around your mundane duties may begin now. You may be considering dropping some of your responsibilities or delegating them elsewhere. If this can be done, you may see a glimpse of a future life with more time to choose what and who you spend time with.

Wednesday 12th

Your emotions are centred around how you appear to others. This may cause you to aim for making big impacts on important people. It may be that you step outside the box and take on a role which is new and exciting. If it aligns with your personal truth, go for it.

Thursday 13th

Money and possessions may be a theme today. You may need to do some networking or learn a new skill to help you manage this. Put your mind to this and you will master it in no time. It may be a juggling act to make things fair.

Friday 14th

Plenty of air energy continues to help you with mental tasks. You could be doing a job for the greater good and getting a lot of satisfaction from it. Your ruler, Venus is giving you some tips about how beautiful harmony and equilibrium can be. She may also bring in the money today.

Saturday 15th

Today you are driven to connect with family members and share the love. You may feel protective of the young or wish to be mothered yourself. Make sure that however you choose, doesn't conflict with others and cause a few triggers to go off. Childhood habits and wounds may reappear.

Sunday 16th

You may desire a familial connection or need meaningful, nurturing conversations. However, this may become cumbersome as you may be coerced into taking on more responsibilities. There may be some guilt involved, but stay strong and say no if others are asking too much. Remember, you are trying to lighten your load.

Monday 17th

It's possible that you experience passive-aggressive behaviour now. Family members or people you deal with in close relationship may be manipulative and demand more of your time and energy than you are comfortable giving. This may be part of your lessons this year. Perfect the art of give and take in relationships.

Tuesday 18th

Speak your truth and stand up for yourself today. You may need to roar louder than usual. Fiery energy helps you to be assertive and make sure that your own needs are met. Be careful that this doesn't lead to hot tempers and harsh words which can't be retracted.

Wednesday 19th

Another challenging day may begin with your good intentions to keep the peace. However, you might bump up against a few restrictions or roadblocks and wish you hadn't bothered. You or someone else could be pretty stubborn and unless someone backs down, this won't be resolved any time today.

Thursday 20th

As your mood lifts, you may wish to try a different approach to achieving peace. Family members may have been able to support you in your downtimes and are now encouraging you to be bold. This may mean that an apology is in order. Accept one or make one.

Friday 21st

This may be a good time to look at your finances. It may be that you have old subscriptions to be renewed or cancelled. You may also have funds invested with another person which need reviewing. Clean up your bank balance and get creative with new money-making ideas.

Saturday 22nd

You may have some ingenious ideas today which you are keen to implement. These may not involve your vision plan or true north. They may, however, include a romantic relationship or a creative project. A switch up or declutter of your working space will make room for new and exciting things.

Sunday 23rd

It's important to check in with your health and your important relationships now. There may be something you have neglected to do which needs urgent attention. Saturn turns direct and lifts restrictions in the workplace. Prepare for some intense partner time as both Venus and the Sun enter your relationship zone.

Monday 24th

Your head and heart are in sync and you can give yourself a good talking to. It's likely that you are reconciling something to yourself or trying to justify some recent action. You can begin the working week with your head held high and a resolution to be responsible.

Tuesday 25th

A new moon and solar eclipse in your relationship area can help you set intentions which may take you to uncharted waters. This could be an intensely, sexy time as Venus is in the mix. Be warned that your dark shadow material is likely to surface, but if you acknowledge it, you may heal it.

Wednesday 26th

Thoughts of past relationships or difficult times may surface. You may try to stuff them back inside, but they continue to play on your mind. They have the potential to throw you right off track, so you need to face them head-on and deal with them respectfully and responsibly.

Thursday 27th

You may have a sleepless night as your mind is wandering and uncontrollable. Try to consider problems from different angles. Illusions and confusion confound you. Wait until you have some clarity. A burst of energy this afternoon may distract you from your worries. Take care and use it wisely.

Friday 28th

Today you may be more outgoing and willing to connect with friends or associates. Supportive groups may be somewhere for you to hide out for the weekend. You could find a guru or leader who can walk and talk you through any psychological issues that keep repeating themselves.

Saturday 29th

Merging and being part of a team or group feels right for you now. You may be able to communicate something you've been struggling with. Reach out to people who are empathic and are familiar with dealing with emotions. You may make deep conversation with a lover this evening.

Sunday 30th

Mars turns retrograde today. This may slow you down and dampen your enthusiasm. Try not to push or move against the flow during this time. Other energy suggests you are outgoing and cheerful. You may have had a weight lifted from your mind and feel at peace.

Monday 31st

Something is ready to be changed or let go of. This may be the remnants of shadow material which you have now healed. Close the door on that particular episode. This may have been a long, hard climb, but you will soon see the benefits of doing your inner work.

NOVEMBER

. . . .

Tuesday 1st

You may have a difficult day at work. This could bring out the
worst in you and people see a side which you would rather
keep hidden in your professional life. Your stubborn side may
not budge, and you could be unwilling to work well with
others. Keep a cool head and don't throw a tantrum.

Wednesday 2nd

Mars hits you with a roadblock and tries to teach you to be
more flexible. There are ways around this, but you may need
someone to point them out. You might desire to switch off and
shut out the world. Problems in your love life may remind you
of the past.

Thursday 3rd

You may find that your emotions are being filtered through a
different lens. The ability to investigate your own deep truths
may bring you to an understanding of why you relate as you
do. If you have some revelations today, be prepared to take on
the advice.

Friday 4th

Your inner compass is in front of you but may be hazy and
confusing. Does it still hold value for you? Are you still
aligned? You may have a period of adjustment to go through
which you feel slows you down. Emotions may be too big to
deal with sensibly today.

Saturday 5th

Drop down into your private thoughts and investigate a few old habits. Your conditioned behaviour may be preventing your growth. Try to learn new ways of responding that are more beneficial to you. This could shake up the dust of old relationships and affect a current one.

Sunday 6th

You could feel the benefit of taking things slowly today. This is your usual default, but if you're told to slow down, you usually do the opposite. Try not to resist a change or ending this evening. Ghosts from the past whisper in your ear and you may need to exorcise them.

Monday 7th

Put your best foot forward today and rejoin society. Problems in relating may affect the quality of your work today. Do your best to get your duties and obligations done before attempting to right any wrongs with a partner. If you want it, do all it takes to get it.

Tuesday 8th

A full moon and lunar eclipse in your sign may close a window on love, money and other heavy issues. This wild card energy may make you unstable and restless today. Say nothing. Listen to and observe what is going on around you.

Wednesday 9th

Be very careful what you say today. You are likely to upset someone, probably a partner. This may stir up some old troubles and bring them back up. You could get a good look at how some of your habits have been preventing you from living the life you want.

Thursday 10th

Setting boundaries or making agreements within relationships may be needed. This won't be easy, but the window is open for you to at least express your thoughts on this. You may be conflicted with what you want from a partner and how that fits in with your life purpose. Work on this now.

Friday 11th

Look at the things or concepts which hold value for you. Are you filling your life up with material things which hold no meaningful connection? You may enjoy your luxuries and special objects, but if real love connection is what you seek, you won't find it within them.

Saturday 12th

Emotions can be strong or overwhelming today. Conversations or trips to family may lead you to spill more of your truth than you would normally. If family are your safety net, then this is fine. Right now, you wish to be nurtured and loved as if you were a child again.

Sunday 13th

Helpful planetary energy is available for you to set a few things straight. Try not to be sucked into illusional or wishful thinking. Love and harmony, when accepted, can make a big difference to you. Be prepared to trawl the depths of your psyche and let go of old stuff.

Monday 14th

Grieving for something you have lost, has expired or outdated is fine. Honour that it had a presence in your life. You may be more able to open up and speak from the heart now. Make sure that it's honest, kind and respectful. You have more courage today to do this.

. . . .

Tuesday 15th

Things are changing and you may need to have an important
talk to a lover today. This may be a turning point and you
will need to pause and carefully consider your options before
proceeding. If you feel stuck, listen to your feelings and that
inner voice. Don't use power to provoke.

Wednesday 16th

If you take your time and remain open and honest, you could
see your relationship deepening. Communication is the key
here, especially letting your partner in on what your dreams
and visions are. They may come on board with you or they may
not, but they will be supportive.

Thursday 17th

You may be in the mood to discover things which are
mysterious, foreign or which appeal to your sensuous side. If
learning new subjects or languages are your thing, now is a
good time. Cultures and philosophies might be a trigger point
for travel and make your world a bit bigger.

Friday 18th

This may simply be a day where you get on with your work and
ignore outside distractions. This evening you could feel them
calling, but know that it isn't the right time to act. You may be
irritated by this, but you can do the things which call later.

Saturday 19th

Do your weekend duties and meet your obligations. You may
leave space to dream and play later on. A feeling of satisfaction
can fill you with pride knowing that you've had a well-balanced
day. Intimacy and deep love await you this evening. Make the
most of it.

Sunday 20th

Mental stimulation may be what you need today. Someone may call upon you to fix a problem or act as an authority figure. Your opinions and advice may be sought after. It's also possible that you're negotiating a deal which will enhance your career. Be someone to look up to now.

Monday 21st

This is an interesting time for love. As the Sun leaves this area, the Moon enters. This may mean that fears or worries surface. However, if the groundwork has been done with the Sun, this won't be a problem. Deep emotional bonding gives you the freedom to talk tonight.

Tuesday 22nd

There is a trigger which keeps coming up and is now screaming for your attention. This has to do with past relationships or times when you had intense feelings or fears. Thinking about this today may cause some tremors inside you and threaten to shift your mood to a negative one.

Wednesday 23rd

Your feelings may be turbulent as you navigate your way through old territory. There's no use in digging up the old unless you intend to dispose of it altogether. Make it into a ritual. Honour the place it once held in your life and let it go with love.

Thursday 24th

Hold out your arms for the many blessings you're about to receive today. Jupiter turns direct and a new moon signals a new and intimate journey. Venus and Mercury are involved too, so discuss what you desire with your partner, pack up and hit the road together.

Friday 25th

There's no need to rush today. You may be trying to attach to your inner compass, but it's evading you. Just enjoy the breath of fresh air and stop pushing against the flow. This evening you might see that your efforts were futile and resolve to be sensible at the next attempt.

Saturday 26th

It's a good weekend to plan effectively for the months to come. You may be itching to travel now, especially with a partner. Use this time to research and make a vision board of what you wish to explore. Broaden your horizons on many different levels and enjoy yourself.

Sunday 27th

Think of the most improbable things you'd like to do and then plan for them. It may be time to break the mould and go beyond your comfort zone. Just be realistic. You might feel completely in control of your life right now and can set about making big ideas.

Monday 28th

You can be fiercely outgoing today. This is great and fills you with optimism, but Mars is asking you to think twice, make sure you are clear and think again. You may come up against a hurdle if you haven't covered all the options. Pause and assess everything in your game plan now.

Tuesday 29th

Your mind may be doing overtime and not letting you rest. Keep your mind on your work or your distractions will be noticed by an authority figure. A course of higher education may fill the gap you have until you can get away and experience things for yourself.

Wednesday 30th

It's possible that your enthusiasm is infecting others in the workplace and your wider circles. If you can pitch some ideas to the boss, you may be able to combine travel with work. You may be getting a spiritual high at this time which helps you put a few things in perspective.

DECEMBER

Thursday 1st

Tread lightly today, the energy suggests you could be easily upset by friends, social groups or lovers. Check finances or investments you have with another person. There may be some disagreements about the value of these now. Be flexible and open to new ideas for managing money.

Friday 2nd

Your empathy may be limitless today, but this can make you tired and you could need alone time. Conversations with a lover may be difficult or border on the taboo. You may wish to consider whether this is in line with your personal truths and inner compass. Remember your own boundaries.

Saturday 3rd

You may be passionate today and wish to see some action. This could involve some deep investigations into your psyche or a deep desire to be intimate with a lover. However, with Mars retrograde, you might find that your own home is the best place to be right now.

Sunday 4th

Neptune turns direct. Using your inner compass, review what you have noticed in past months. Have illusions faded away? Have you taken off the rose-coloured spectacles? You may have a crisis of conscience now and realise that something you have invested deeply in, is not as it once seemed.

Monday 5th

Today you may have an overwhelming desire for truth. It's possible that you feel that you've wasted time and no longer know what is right for you. This energy will pass so don't dwell on it too much. Look to the future and start shaking things up. Find your inner rebel.

Tuesday 6th

Conversations may reveal a truth or deception. You might be shocked at first, but when you have had time to process it, you may be relieved. All eyes are on you, so ensure that your responses are adult and responsible. Take stock of what brings you joy and quality now.

Wednesday 7th

Take time to gather your thoughts and be at peace with yourself. If your mind wanders, let it. Try not to fixate on one thing as you may reverse your thinking in the future. Learning about what you value is an important lesson as it also teaches you what you don't want.

Thursday 8th

Today's full moon may spotlight exactly what you treasure and need around you. As Mars is also there, you may feel irritable or find it hard to accept some losses. Put your mind to your work and do your tasks. Practical and mental activities will distract from your emotions.

Friday 9th

Putting up your defences may not be a good idea now. Instead, try being vulnerable and allowing close relatives, especially maternal types to comfort you. Good home-cooked food and familiar habits are needed now. Nourish your soul and let others care for you. Get into your safety zone.

Saturday 10th

You may have a yearning to start something different now. A course of higher education may attract you. Travel could be on your mind. Choose something in which you can go at your own pace. The wider world is waiting for you. Make a plan.

Sunday 11th

Change may be difficult today, so make it small. It could simply be that you leave the company of a carer or close friend for now. Emotional energy is carrying you along and you may not be comfortable with this. By evening, you may find your voice and make it count.

Monday 12th

You have a good sense of duty and responsibility today and this will be noticed by those above you. Challenges may present themselves this evening as you may be recalling past loves and intimate moments. These must stay in the past as they aren't going to help you now.

Tuesday 13th

Being stubborn and wanting your own way is not a good look. You may be fighting anyone who crosses your path today and coming across as childish or defiant. Use that fiery energy to do something productive. Get out the maps and think about a dream holiday to plan.

Wednesday 14th

Grounding energy gives you some relief today. You're at your best when doing practical activity. Try getting creative or decluttering a messy area. This could also be a time to detox your body ready for the heavy festive season. Be good to yourself today and get some quality self-care.

Thursday 15th

The good energy continues to keep you occupied with worthwhile pursuits. If you experience a sudden blockage or tiredness, don't stress about it. It will resolve itself this afternoon and the breakthrough may give you a great deal of satisfaction. You may even rebel a little or invent something. Congratulate or reward yourself.

Friday 16th

There may be no time for dreaming today as your inner compass evades you. Perhaps there is too much to do and your mundane duties are piling up. This may get you down a little, but these are necessary jobs and need to be done. Deadlines may be calling you.

Saturday 17th

Balance will not be easily achieved today. You may need to delegate some jobs or ask for help. Weekend fun may come, but there may be a lot to do first. When it does, let your hair down and have fun. You may be outrageous today at an early festive party.

Sunday 18th

This may be another day where you are needed to make preparations or just show up and say your piece. There may be decisions where your opinion is valued. If this interferes with your free time you may need to sit tight, get on with it and do your duty.

Monday 19th

Love is on the agenda today as your special relationships are harmonic and pleasing. You may get something now which you have been yearning for recently. Shared dreams and passions make it easier for you to relate to a partner. Maybe you are planning a trip together.

Tuesday 20th

A little loving can go a long way today. Mutual respect and joy with a partner can provide you with a sense of inner peace. The future looks brighter and you are ready to begin the journey towards it. You may have matured in a relationship or the relationship itself has evolved.

Wednesday 21st

The winter solstice arrives to lead you into the darker nights. Choose to use this day to pause, reflect and give gratitude for the year gone by. It suits you to schedule activities that take you deeper into yourself and others that explore the wider world.

Thursday 22nd

As the festive days approach quickly, you may find you are more tired than usual. It would help if you aimed to co-operate and not make your own agenda. You may wish to switch up the normal or traditional ways of doing things. Be respectful to all you share this time with.

Friday 23rd

A new moon is a great opportunity to make plans for things which have several steps and may take a long time to achieve. Slowly suits you, as you're aware. You may be asked to take a leadership role now or in the New Year. Consider if this aligns with your journey.

Saturday 24th

This is a great day for conversations which reach out to touch the heart of another. It's an emotional day but filled with promise and hope for a bright future. Your inner rebel is itching to come out and this may just be the party animal getting ready.

Sunday 25th

Self-control is important today. You may be hosting the celebrations, but if you aren't, you need to let another shine. You are more altruistic than usual and may enjoy the peace this gives you deep inside. A heart filled with optimism is a heart worth sharing with others.

Monday 26th

Today may present small challenges and will almost certainly be about relating to others. You might need more time alone, but your obligations prevent this. Try not to show any resentment and play your role in the family today. Remember personal boundaries and remain respectful. Pitch in and do your bit.

Tuesday 27th

Friends and social groups have your attention now. Perhaps an escape to your soul tribe is needed. Your empathy is strong, and you may wish to merge with like-minded folk either online or in your community. Ethereal energy helps you to be hopeful, flexible and part of a loving circle.

Wednesday 28th

You may be in exactly the right frame of mind to connect to your inner compass. There is a good chance that you feel more connected now than all year. Your dreams and intentions seem aligned and ready for you to approach. Start that journey now and remember this feeling.

Thursday 29th

Mercury turns retrograde to see the year out. You may need to be more adaptable now. Remember to back up devices and make communication crystal clear. Love talk may experience misunderstanding today, but if you're aware of Mercury's tricks, you can be more meticulous when speaking, planning and travelling.

Friday 30th

The holiday season may have worn you out and today you feel its effects. To save your energy for another party, take a day to yourself or on the sofa with favourite movies. Don't commit to visitors if you don't have the energy. If you do, you may get irritable.

Saturday 31st

Challenging energy ends the year and you may not be in the mood to celebrate. You could be feeling manipulated or coerced into something you're unsure of. You may even feel trapped by the confines of family and friends or had enough of partying. Do the right thing and retreat if you're overwhelmed.

Taurus

. . . .

PEOPLE WHO
YOUR SIGN

PEOPLE WHO
SHARE YOUR SIGN

· · · · · · · · · · · · · · · · ·

Ambitious Taureans dominate in their professional fields, and their tenacity has seen many rise to fame throughout history and in the present day. From famous singers like Adele and Ella Fitzgerald, to top models such as Gigi Hadid and renowned artists like Salvador Dalí, the beauty that Taureans bring into the world is evident. Discover the creative Taureans who share your exact birthday and see if you can spot any similarities.

21st April

Jessey Stevens (1992), James McAvoy (1979), Steve Backshall (1973), Robert Smith (1959), Iggy Pop (1947), Diana Darvey (1945), Queen Elizabeth II of the United Kingdom (1926), Charlotte Brontë (1816)

22nd April

Louis Smith (1989), Tyra Sanchez (1988), Michelle Ryan (1984), Daniel Johns (1973), Jack Nicholson (1937), Glen Campbell (1936), Immanuel Kant (1724), Queen Isabella I of Castile (1451)

23rd April

Gigi Hadid (1995), Taio Cruz (1980), Jaime King (1979), John Cena (1977), Kal Penn (1977), Michael Moore (1954), Sandra Dee (1942), Shirley Temple (1928), Dorian Leigh (1917), James Buchanan, U.S. President (1791), William Shakespeare (1564)

24th April

Casper Lee (1994), Joe Keery (1992), Kelly Clarkson (1982), Austin Nichols (1980), Cedric the Entertainer (1964), Barbra Streisand (1942), Shirley MacLaine (1934)

25th April

Joslyn Davis (1982), Alejandro Valverde (1980), Tim Duncan (1976), Renée Zellweger (1969), Hank Azaria (1964), Len Goodman (1944), Al Pacino (1940), Ella Fitzgerald (1917), Oliver Cromwell (1599)

26th April

Luke Bracey (1989), Jemima Kirke (1985), Channing Tatum (1980), Melania Trump (1970), Kevin James (1965), Giancarlo Esposito (1958), Roger Taylor (1949), Carol Burnett (1933)

27th April

Froy Gutierrez (1998), Jenna Coleman (1986), Patrick Stump (1984), Darcey Bussell (1969), Tess Daly (1969), Coretta Scott King (1927), Ulysses S. Grant, U.S. President (1822)

28th April

Melanie Martinez (1995), Jessica Alba (1981), Penélope Cruz (1974), Bridget Moynahan (1971), Diego Simeone (1970), Jay Leno (1950), Terry Pratchett (1948), Harper Lee (1926), Oskar Schindler (1908), James Monroe, U.S. President (1758)

29th April

Katherine Langford (1996), Kian Egan (1980), Uma Thurman (1970), Kolinda Grabar-Kitarović, Croatian President (1968), Michelle Pfeiffer (1958), Daniel Day-Lewis (1957), Jerry Seinfeld (1954), Willie Nelson (1933)

30th April

Travis Scott (1992), Dianna Agron (1986), Gal Gadot (1985), Kirsten Dunst (1982), Kunal Nayyar (1981), Johnny Galecki (1975), Leigh Francis (1973), Queen Juliana of the Netherlands (1909)

1st May

Caggie Dunlop (1989), Anushka Sharma (1988), Leonardo Bonucci (1987), Jamie Dornan (1982), James Murray (1976), Wes Anderson (1969), Tim McGraw (1967), Joanna Lumley (1946), Calamity Jane (1852)

2nd May

Lily Allen (1985), Ellie Kemper (1980), David Beckham (1975), Dwayne Johnson (1972), Donatella Versace (1955), Christine Baranski (1952), James Dyson (1947), Catherine the Great (1729)

3rd May

MC Pedrinho (2002), Poppy Delevingne (1986), Rebecca Hall (1982), Eric Church (1977), Christina Hendricks (1975), Rob Brydon (1965), Frankie Valli (1934), James Brown (1933)

4th May

Alex Lawther (1995), Rory McIlroy (1989), Radja Nainggolan (1988), Francesc Fàbregas (1987), Trisha Krishnan (1983), Will Arnett (1970), Keith Haring (1958), Mick Mars (1951), Audrey Hepburn (1929)

5th May

Brooke Hogan (1988), Adele (1988), Bart Baker (1986), Henry Cavill (1983), Craig David (1981), Vincent Kartheiser (1979), Karl Marx (1818)

6th May

Mateo Kovačić (1994), Naomi Scott (1993), Meek Mill (1987), Chris Paul (1985), Dani Alves (1983), George Clooney (1961), Orson Welles (1915), Sigmund Freud (1856)

7th May

Alexander Ludwig (1992), Earl Thomas (1989), Chiara Ferragni (1987), J Balvin (1985), Breckin Meyer (1974), Michael Rosen (1946), Pyotr Ilyich Tchaikovsky (1840), Johannes Brahms (1833)

8th May

Katy B (1989), Nyle DiMarco (1989), Matt Willis (1983), Stephen Amell (1981), Matthew Davis (1978), Enrique Iglesias (1975), David Attenborough (1926), Harry S. Truman, U.S. President (1884)

9th May

Noah Centineo (1996), Audrina Patridge (1985), Rosario Dawson (1979), Ghostface Killah (1970), John Corbett (1961), Billy Joel (1949), Candice Bergen (1946), Albert Finney (1936)

10th May

Halston Sage (1993), Lindsey Shaw (1989), Aslı Enver (1984), Linda Evangelista (1965), Bono (1960), Ellen Ochoa (1958), Sid Vicious (1957), Fred Astaire (1899)

11th May

Sabrina Carpenter (1999), Lana Condor (1997), Thibaut Courtois (1992), Blac Chyna (1988), Holly Valance (1983), Cory Monteith (1982), Jonathan Jackson (1982), Salvador Dalí (1904)

12th May

Emily VanCamp (1986), Domhnall Gleeson (1983), Malin Åkerman (1978), Jason Biggs (1978), Tony Hawk (1968), Catherine Tate (1968), Emilio Estevez (1962), Florence Nightingale (1820)

13th May

Debby Ryan (1993), Romelu Lukaku (1993), Tommy Dorfman (1992), Robert Pattinson (1986), Iwan Rheon (1985), Yaya Touré (1983), Stevie Wonder (1950), Joe Louis (1914)

14th May

Martin Garrix (1996), Miranda Cosgrove (1993), Dustin Lynch (1985), Olly Murs (1984), Mark Zuckerberg (1984), Martine McCutcheon (1976), Cate Blanchett (1969), Greg Davies (1968), George Lucas (1944)